# Dancing with Trees

# Dancing with Trees
## A Family Journal

## Benny Graves

SARTORIS
LITERARY
GROUP

A traditional publisher with a non-traditional approach to publishing

SARTORIS LITERARY GROUP
Metro-Jackson, Mississippi
**www.sartorisliterary.com**

To my wife, Deanie, who is my constant inspiration

# CONTENTS

Photo by istock.com/bennygraves

# Dancing with Trees

**Three Oaks still stand / Photo by Benny Graves**

# Chapter 1

## Testaments of Love

I know something about love. I've seen it.

In 1949, my Dad, a World War II veteran, had recently married my mother. As newlyweds in their 20's, they lived in a small college town in Mississippi, in a tiny upstairs, two-room apartment. That first summer was sweltering hot. Somehow they endured the heat with the aid of a single box fan Dad was able to purchase. They knew the hot, cramped little apartment wouldn't be conducive to raising a family. Before long, Dad convinced Mother to relocate to the farm where he grew up. She followed him home because she loved him.

The newlyweds started the transition by building a modest 1500-square foot house directly across the road from his parents' home on a parcel of the family land. They secured a loan for building materials from a wealthy local businessman because the town bank would not consider taking a chance on a young couple just starting out. The total cost of the house was $1,700. Money was scarce, but their love was strong.

After the frame house was completed, Dad planted three water oak saplings in front of their new home. He dug the young trees up from the big woods on the backside of the farm and lined them up along the road with two on one side of the driveway and one on the other. Together, the newlyweds faithfully watered the little oaks that first summer to help the trees survive the heat and dry spells of the Deep South. They spent a lifetime involved in shared activities like this; they were inseparable. Naturally, planting the trees was a practical decision. Dad knew the western exposure of their house would need protection from the sun. Of course, air conditioning did not exist in their world in 1949.

As the trees grew, so did their family. One by one, four little children came along—three girls and me, a skinny, redheaded boy.

I grew up with the three oak trees. In fact, I've lived my whole life in the shadows of these oaks. The trio stood watch, providing a fast-growing canopy as we played games of hide-and-seek, chase, and baseball. My family shared plenty of love and laughter under these trees.

From under these oaks, I watched Mother kiss Dad good-bye each day at the front door as he left for work. Then, in the evening, when he returned, all of us kids would rush him as he entered the house, each one of us vying for his attention. Mother would slip her hand in his and retreat with him into our only bathroom and shut the door—just to have a moment of privacy with the man she loved. Through the door, she would tell us all to go outside and play. We kids could never understand why they would want to be separated from us to spend time whispering in some ole bathroom.

During hot Mississippi summers, my sisters and I sold lemonade to those who passed by on the road. Under the shade of the mighty oaks, we set up our business on a square card table and charged a nickel for a cup. Mother would keep an eye on us through the window.

On some days, I climbed these sturdy trees and felt like captain of the world atop their highest branches. On one occasion, I found a blue jay's nest, and bursting with excitement, I raced to tell Mother and Dad about the speckled eggs. Mother gave me a hug; Dad smiled and told me to be careful up there in those trees.

Late one particular evening, I plopped down on the grass and leaned against the trunk of one of these oaks beside the driveway. It was a warm summer night, and I waited under the tree's watchful awning for Dad to return home from working late. When he arrived, he found me asleep. Then, he scooped me up in his arms, gently carried me into the house, and laid me in my bed.

Most of the time I took these trees for granted. They were just there as part of our landscape. We used them to tack up yard sale signs or as landmarks to tell someone directions to our house. As my sisters and I learned to drive, we learned to be extra careful when backing our long station wagon out of our driveway, as to not hit a tree with the car. My baby sister when she was a senior in high school even taught Mother to drive. Mother was fifty-four when she got her driver's license. Somehow, the trees survived.

Through the years, the trees grew into massive oaks, which on hot summer days cast a fine shade on a small, white house. Within sight of the big oaks across the street, my parents tended a vegetable garden for over fifty years. They passed the time working the garden in quiet conversation. Their hard work was rewarded with an abundance of beautiful produce. No one knows how many people were fed by the vegetables they gave away. It was their way of showing they cared. The water oaks witnessed this old couple holding hands each day as they walked back home holding buckets of tomatoes or peas. A trailing pet cat followed. Theirs was a strong, special love.

As they aged, I checked on them daily. Walking up to their house, I knew the scene I would see inside: Mother's small rocker inches away from Dad's recliner; there they sat beside each other, always within touching distance. Many nights, as I entered their house, I'd hear giggles. When I'd asked what they were laughing about, they would look at each other and smile. Mother would say, "Oh, just something we remembered that happened a long time ago."

Later, when Dad was in his nineties, he would sit in his recliner by the window and watch the squirrels frolic in these magnificent oaks. Often, when visitors dropped by, he would retell the story about how the trees came to be in the front yard. When he got to the part about how he and Mother planted the small saplings together, his voice filled with love.

For sixty-seven years of marriage on Earth, Dad and Mother loved each other and their family. My sisters and I saw true love in action every day. Those small saplings they planted in the first year of marriage grew strong and tall and witnessed all the joys and struggles this couple and their family experienced. Both Mother and Dad are gone now, but the three oaks still stand today as a visual testament of their love for each other.

Three massive water oaks growing old in the front yard of an abandoned house may not have much meaning to the folks driving by in their fast cars, but they sure hold many special memories to me. They are true monuments to one couple's enduring love.

"When I was a boy I first learned how much better water tastes when it has set a while in a cedar bucket. Warmish-cool, with a faint taste like the hot July wind in cedar trees smells."
William Faulkner, As I Lay Dying

Photo by Benny Graves

Seven Sisters / Photo by Benny Graves

# Chapter 2

## Working and Playing Together as a Family

Beyond the Seven Sisters, across the pond between distant trees on the horizon, a yellowish full moon begins to rise. Big and round, the mystical half orb slowly climbs in the eastern sky as the light of day slowly fades. Like a nail to a magnet, the scene captures my attention. In an instant, the bucket I'm carrying becomes my front row seat as I pause to soak up this great performance of the heavens.  Within moments, a huge perfect sphere hangs suspended just above the trees, an ancient sign of the rhythm of time. Sitting on a bucket, alone in the silent moonlight, I feel the beat of my heart. I see my breath rise in the cool evening air, and I realize I'm living and breathing exactly where I'm meant to be … on a small Mississippi farm with trees all around.

**\*\*\*\***

With time, my childhood family grew until our tiny white house bustled with seven people. Yes, seven! Dad and Mother, Grandmother BB, three lively girls, and me. As I think back, seven really was a perfect number. Every square inch of our family's house was lived in. Fun and adventure filled that tiny house. The experience of growing up together in the cramped white house still echoes in my life today. What great times we shared!

Since our home was full, we often spilled out into the backyard under the cool shade of seven giant pecan trees. Planted in a straight single file line, the trees progressed through our backyard like guardian soldiers and marched into the adjoining cow pasture. These beautiful trees have been a part of our family for at least five generations. I call them the "Seven Sisters."

In one of my earliest childhood memories, I am lying on a patchwork quilt on a summer day. I can still picture the view as I look up at sunlight dancing in and out of lush green leaves swaying back and forth in the warm breeze.

These seven trees watched over us kids as we played and played and played. We spent hours enjoying simple toys, playing with them in the dirt around their huge trunks. Under the watchful eye of these trees, my sisters taught me how to make mud pies. We carefully patted out each one and dried it in the sun. My oldest sister would use a fork to decorate them with crosshatches just like Mother's pies. I thought they tasted delicious! Well, not really — one bite was all I needed to know that they were nothing like Mother's pies, but what great fun we had in those days.

Dad fastened a long, handmade swing from a sturdy limb, and the sounds of squealing, laughing children filled the air as we swung back and forth. We played for hours until Mother called us inside to supper. Oh how vivid the memories! Back then, a chicken pen with a white henhouse sat under one of the pecan trees in the corner of the backyard. We heard the hens cackle each day as they announced the laying of their eggs. We watched amazed as the birds raced each other every time a poor grasshopper or cricket strayed into the danger zone of the pen. The trees provided shade for the henhouse so we could enjoy fresh eggs for breakfast and fried chicken for Sunday dinner.

Under the shade of the Seven Sisters, our family joined with our black friends, Inez and Mary, to shell peas and shuck sweet corn amid rich stories told by the old folks. Youngsters nearby soaked up much more than words. Around a well-worn picnic table, the trees supervised family picnics, reunions, and watermelon cuttings.

Often in the late fall, these massive trees bore a huge crop of tasty pecans. As the nuts started dropping, we gathered them from among the fallen leaves. It was a family affair filled with a flurry of activity. I can still see Mother sitting on the ground, filling up a dishpan with pecans. We usually started gathering during the clear, pleasant days of early November. However, I also recall picking up pecans during some cold, wet days of December. We'd then take the damp nuts into the house and dry them in big metal pans over the hot floor furnace grate.

One year, after a particularly large pecan crop, Dad sacked up our family's harvest in large burlap bags and carried them in our 1956 International pickup to a sheller/buyer in a distant town. Soon afterward, we found shiny new bicycles under our Christmas tree. We were all thrilled beyond belief. Dad made sure his children knew that everyone's hard work had made it possible for Santa to provide those bikes. Through experiences like this, our parents taught us the value of hard work and the power of working together as a family.

Later, when my own two daughters were growing up, I made sure we all shared time as a family picking up pecans under the Seven Sisters.   I have tried to pass on the lessons of life and the value of work and family. Those times together with my girls gathering pecans brought me great pleasure—the depth of which only the Seven Sisters can understand.

Last Tree Before Home /  Photo by Benny Graves

# Chapter 3

## Calm Assurance

The screen door slammed on the back porch as a fresh, redheaded boy charged out to engage the warm summer day. The little white house could not contain this five-year-old a minute longer. The feel of fresh grass on his bare feet was pure joy, which only served to energize the boy's will to explore beyond the backyard fence for the first time. Over the fence, he climbed to land with a thud in the north pasture. A vast new world lay before him. At that very moment, an all-knowing mother burst from the house to caution her little boy.

"Puhlease, Mother. I wanna go esplorin.' Please," he begged in his sweetest voice.

She sensed his intense need for freedom and independence, and with a loud exhale, she replied, "Okay. Go play, but stay within the fence of the pasture."

"I will. I promise," he yelled eagerly before he took off running.

"You come in when I call you for lunch," she yelled after him.

"Yes, mam!" he hollered back.

From the perspective of a five-year-old boy, the little twenty-acre farm pasture looked like the ocean, full of adventure and the mysterious unknown. Tall grass swaying in the breeze like waves on the ocean and trees dotting the horizon like islands were all waiting to be discovered.

As he began his adventure, the first tree he came to on the fence line was a large sweet gum tree with multiple trunks. Naturally, he had to climb the tree, at least to its lowest limbs. There, he discovered green spiked seed balls suspended from leafy twigs. To him, these were strange, new objects.  Collecting a few, he shoved them into his pants pockets to look at later with a flashlight under his bedsheets.

The next day, while scouting farther up the fence line, he encountered his first catalpa tree loaded with black and yellow worms, happily munching on its heart shaped leaves. What a wonder!   He picked up a stick to poke at a fallen worm. On his hands and knees, he got his face as close as he could to the worm so he could examine every detail of this bizarre new creature. He couldn't wait to describe his strange discovery to Mother over lunch.

With each passing day, he gained confidence in his explorations and pushed farther and farther away from his house. The boy navigated all across the pasture, always using the perimeter fence as his lifeline. The sweet gum tree would confirm he was back close to home.

 One day, he found himself on the far side of the pasture. There, he saw three small-frame houses just beyond the fence on the other side of a dusty dirt road. As he came by the third house, a little black boy came to the fence to greet him.  The boy was smaller than him and was looking down at his bare feet. He had some wooden toy cars in his hands.

Finally, the redheaded boy asked, "Where did you get those cars?"

The black boy said, "My cousin found 'em but they mine now. Wanna see how fast they go?"

Soon the redheaded boy had crawled under the barbed wire and was playing in the dirt of his new friend's front yard. As they played, the boys talked and found out they were the same age.

Suddenly, the redheaded boy heard some yapping and asked, pointing under the house, "You got puppies back there?"

"Sure do. Three black ones and two brown ones. Come on and you can hold 'em." The boy led the way to the edge of the front porch. They squatted down and called under the house. To their delight, the little puppies came running.

Over the next few days, they saw each other regularly and became fast friends and playmates. They met daily at the fence in front of the boy's house. Summer days drifted by as the buddies played and explored the world together.

Each day, his mother's call would echo across the pasture, and the redheaded boy knew it was time to go. After saying good-bye to his friend, he would follow the fence line back down the hill and around till he came to the old gum tree, the last tree before home. The tree was a steadfast landmark that gave him a measure of calm assurance. Every time he passed the old tree, he gave it a couple of pats with his hand, for he knew he had made it once again safely back home.

These boys, who met that summer, grew up together. They attended school together, played football together, and eventually graduated high school.  After graduation, they parted, and the flow of life took them in different directions. The years hurried by like pages of a good book.

****

Late in the evening, a gray haired man wearing a ragged straw hat walked slowly down a hill as he mended the rusty barbed wire of a pasture fence.  He passed the old home place of his long ago playmate. The house had been torn down years ago, and now only a pile of rotten boards remained where it once stood. A few steps farther, he peeked up at the catalpa tree hoping to see a worm. Finally, after following the fence up a small rise, he arrived at the last tree on the fence line, an old sweet gum. He reached out his weathered hand and gave the tree a couple of pats on its trunk. Pausing a moment, he looked toward his childhood home, and then slowly moved on into the twilight.

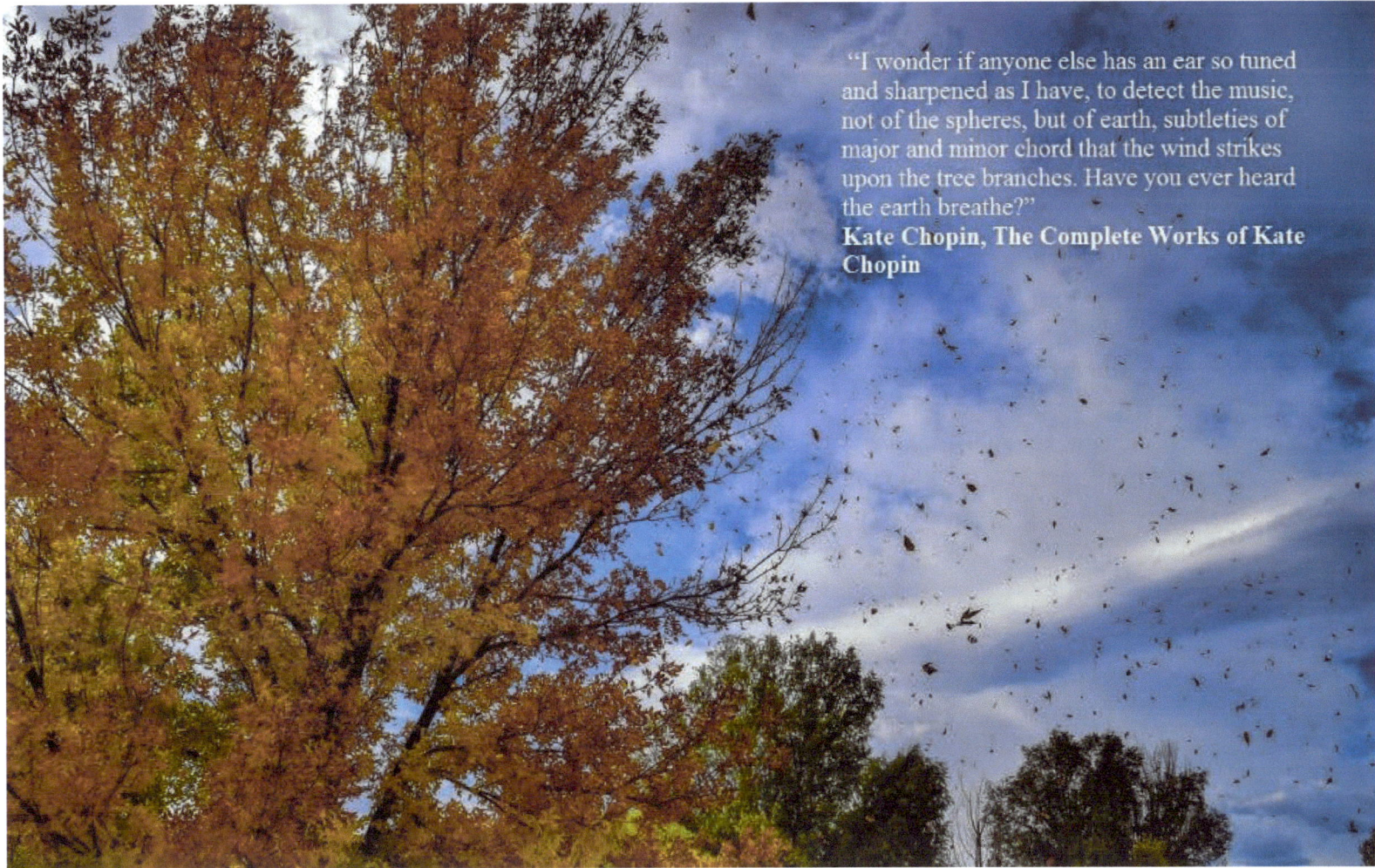

"I wonder if anyone else has an ear so tuned and sharpened as I have, to detect the music, not of the spheres, but of earth, subtleties of major and minor chord that the wind strikes upon the tree branches. Have you ever heard the earth breathe?"
**Kate Chopin, The Complete Works of Kate Chopin**

hoto by istock.com/bennygraves

25

The Persimmon Tree / Photo by Benny Graves

# Chapter 4

## Self-Control

Hidden behind a small grove of oaks in the far corner of the north pasture, a single persimmon tree grows. A slender, unassuming medium sized tree, it has gone unnoticed by most people who have passed by it over the years. However, I have noticed this tree and have found it bears an abundance of soft, orange fruit every year.

In the fall when its aromatic fruit ripens, this overlooked tree suddenly becomes a magnet, drawing all sorts of wildlife in the area. Raccoons, possums, skunks, red foxes, coyotes, wild turkeys, and crows have all feasted on its juicy persimmons during the months of late autumn. The whitetail deer on the farm especially love these orange, round treats and visit the tree regularly. Every deer in the surrounding area of the farm seems to know exactly when the first fruit drops. I enjoy watching these creatures of the wild as they are drawn to this lone persimmon tree.

During my childhood, at about the age of eight, I took my first overnight camping trip outside the backyard. My pal and I pitched our Sears and Roebuck pup tent late one summer evening under the persimmon tree. We thought we were something to be camping in the wilds of the north pasture, out of sight of the house and our parents. We carefully set up our green canvas tent, gathered some firewood, and built a crackling fire. We were doing just fine until the darkness of night fell.

Then, somewhere out in the spooky shadows just beyond the flickering firelight, strange noises pierced our nerves. The screeching of an owl followed by the sound of rustling leaves in the blackness of a moonless night can get a young boy's attention like nothing else. We stayed awake most of the night and kept a roaring fire burning bright, not daring to close our eyes until fatigue finally overtook us at dawn.

Roused by the sweltering heat of the morning sun on thick canvas, we crawled out, stretched, and ate our breakfast of graham crackers smeared with peanut butter. We washed it all down with a Dixie cup of Tang.

Then, my buddy discovered green persimmons hanging above our tent. I stood on my friend's shoulders to pick several big handfuls. As young boys do, we dared each other to bite into one of the unripen fruits at the same time. On the count of three, we took a bite. I believe everyone should experience the "pucker power" of a fresh green persimmon. We laughed until it hurt when we saw the awful face each other made. After much spitting and gagging, the feeling finally came back to my mouth. I was so proud that I had survived the dare. What great times to be a country boy in the summer under the persimmon tree!

Wild animals were not the only ones on the farm drawn to the ripening persimmons. Back then, we had a huge old Hereford bull. He was red with a white face and had a red bullseye on his right eye. This old bull took a real liking to the special fruit of this tree.

On one particular fall morning, my Dad gave me the chore of counting the cows and reporting to him before he left for work. As I counted the animals, I soon learned the old Hereford bull was nowhere to be found. He was not with the cows, so I looked and looked for him. I searched all the pastures, creeks, and woodlots with no luck. Finally, in the very back of the north pasture behind a grove of oaks, I found the red beast standing alone under the persimmon tree. He had obviously been standing there for days waiting for one more tasty orange fruit to drop.

I remember Dad saying the crazy old bull had gotten addicted to the sweet persimmons and was willing to starve to death waiting under that tree.

"Let that be a lesson to you, boy," my dad said. "You gotta have some self-control."

Looking at the gaunt creature, it was evident that the bull had already lost weight. Together, Dad and I drove the poor bull to the barn lot and closed the gate to keep him away from his temptation.

To this day, the persimmon tree continues to bear fruit each fall.  As I work around the farm, I instinctively look toward this tree whenever I can, hoping to catch a glimpse of its latest visitor. And I often think about that old bull and smile, remembering Dad's simple but wise advice about self-control.

The Last Tree Standing / Photo by Benny Graves

# Chapter 5

## Disappointment to Joy

In the very back corner of the pasture, a single pecan tree has a story.

From the beginning, education was always one of Mother and Dad's top priorities for their children. In retrospect, I know my parents struggled to figure out how to afford college for all four children. After discussing this situation with his younger brother Clint Jr., who was a professor at the University, Dad came up with the idea of planting a pecan orchard. The idea was to plant the whole north pasture with young pecan trees, and with a little time, these trees would bear pecans and generate much-needed extra income to help with college expenses for us children.

Uncle Clint secured 120 grafted pecan seedlings from Bass Pecan Nursery down in South Mississippi and delivered them to the farm in late winter. Then the real work began. As a young boy, I was beside Dad as we hand-dug each hole two feet deep with a posthole digger. Together, we placed a young tree in each hole, carefully backfilling with good, rich topsoil. Planted in a precise grid pattern, the young orchard looked like money in the bank.

The following summer turned out especially hot, and a drought seized the land. Our young pecan trees were stressed to their breaking point. Dad immediately called the whole family into action to try to save the young trees. For days and weeks that summer, each of us worked hauling water. We filled ten-gallon milk cans, loaded them onto a farm wagon, and used our old Model M John Deere tractor to pull it through the field. One by one, we watered each tree, trying desperately to keep them alive. The next summer, the same drought happened again, so we followed the same routine, but we also had to hoe and pull out the weeds from around the base of each tree. That was our summer vacation.

Dad and Mother and all of us kids worked mighty hard in the new pecan orchard those first few years to do everything possible to keep those trees alive. In spite of our best efforts, one by one, the trees started dying. Eventually every single tree died except one way back over the hill in the back corner. I know it had to be disheartening for Dad and Mother to watch their dream of a successful pecan orchard slowly disappear.

But you know, thinking back, I never remember Dad or Mother showing any outward sign of discouragement about this failure. We just moved on as a family and worked harder at other things on the farm — things like milking cows, raising a huge garden, bottle feeding extra calves, cutting short stick pulpwood, and doing anything we could to make or save a few dollars for the family needs and our future college expenses.

With time, one by one, each of us went off to college. We all paid for our college education by working odd jobs or earning small scholarships. Dad and Mother helped each of us with a little of our expenses as best they could. We did whatever it took to get our education, and I can assure you none of us children wasted any money during our college experience. Money was hard to come by, and it was ingrained in us from birth to work hard and be frugal with our money. As it turned out, we all did just fine; we all got our education, made lifelong friends, and enjoyed our time in college.

Of the four children, I was the one who came back home to the farm, to care for the land and to raise a family. One crisp clear day in late November, I walked hand in hand with my two young daughters to the back corner of the north pasture to gather pecans under a beautiful tall pecan tree loaded with nuts. Laughter rang across the field as the girls rustled through fallen leaves, racing to find big fat pecans. They dropped them by the handful into a five gallon bucket.  It was then I realized that the disappointment of a long ago failed dream had somehow become transformed into pure joy under the last tree standing. We left for home with our bucket filled.

The Hickory Tree and the Gap / Photo by Benny Graves

# Chapter 6

## Facing Adversity

A fine looking hickory tree grows a little distance south of our rustic old dairy barn. With a thick, stout trunk and a broad classic shaped crown, it stands out as a true example of nature's artwork in a pastoral landscape. It provides a cool oasis of deep shade in the heat of summer for all who seek shelter from a scorching sun. The frost of late fall turns the leaves into a masterpiece of pure golden yellow. Its colorful leaves rustle in the light autumn breeze and eventually float to the ground below. Fat hickory nuts lure a single red fox squirrel to carefully scamper across the open pasture each day to harvest the bounty. The squirrel's handiwork of peeled husks and cut hulls lay scattered on the ground at the base of the tree. The rusty barbed wire of an old fence nailed to the hardwood tree many years ago, disappears deep into its trunk, slowly embedded with the passing of time into the very heart of the tree. An old metal gate hangs on the opposite side of the trunk. All my life I have passed this tree, opening and closing the gate, while observing the hickory in all of its glory.

As a little boy, I followed my Dad as he opened that gate under the hickory tree and pushed it aside. We went through the gap together a million times to feed and check on the cows. Dad would always holler in his very loud, distinctive voice to the cows grazing down in the bottom to come get their feed.

I remember the first time he handed me his wooden cow stick and told me to stand in the gate opening and not let any cow come through the gate while he went back into the barn to get some hay. I felt all grown up and very confident as he left me alone. About that time, the old lead cow down in the pasture threw her head up and saw me standing there with the gate wide open. She knew it was feeding time. Immediately, that big mama cow alerted the whole herd with a bellow and proceeded to lead them all at a fast trot, straight for the opening. Standing in the gap with nothing but a stick, I watched wide-eyed as this thundering herd of snorting, bellowing cows approached at a dead run. I tried my best to drag the sagging gate shut, but it was way too heavy for me to move.

My young heart raced with a mixture of adrenaline and fear! I turned to face the cows with my stick held high. The galloping demons were bearing down straight for me. I could feel the ground shake and see the clods of mud flying up from their hooves as they got closer and closer. In a split second, all my confidence evaporated, and my feet told me to turn and run. Just then, I felt the strong, steady hand of my Dad on my shoulder. In a calm voice he said, "Stand still, Son; we'll turn this stampede together." And we did.

It is funny what you remember from your youth. Even today, as I pass this impressive hickory tree, I think about the many life lessons I learned from my Dad as we lived and worked together on the farm—lessons like treating all people with respect, enjoying the simple things of life, appreciating the value of a good name, and experiencing the joy of honest hard work. However, one of the most important lessons I learned from Dad was how to face adversity. He taught me to rely on a steadfast faith which assures me that I am never alone when tough times arise.

Today, when facing the thundering demons of life, I can stand firm in the gap because I know my Heavenly Father stands with me. I feel His hand on my shoulder. The old hickory tree reminds me of this confidence each time I open the gate under its spreading limbs.

"Let's take our hearts for a walk in the woods and listen to the magic whispers of old trees."

**Author Unknown**

Photo by istock.com/bennygraves

The Sycamore Tree / Photo by Benny Graves

# Chapter 7

## Conquer Your Fears

Only one sycamore tree grows on the farm—a striking, multi-trunk tree that stands in a pasture close to one of our creeks. Pure white bark covers the upper trunk and branches, progressing down the tree until it falls off in irregular patches, which exposes patterns of brown, green, and gray bark. This patchy pattern of bark is unique to sycamore trees. Strips of bark cast off during the growing process litter the ground below the tree. With a background of dark green cedars, this particular sycamore is a striking specimen. During summer, large pointed green leaves broader than two hands grace the tree. In fall, after the leaves have fallen, hundreds of round seed balls dangle from bare winter twigs. They swing in the breeze suspended on slender stems like miniature Christmas ornaments.

As I walked by this tree recently, I noticed several fallen branches lying on the ground after a passing thunderstorm. Stooping low, I picked up a crooked, slender white limb, just the right size for a walking stick. A vague feeling of familiarity came over me. I pondered, where had I seen this white stick before? Resting at the base of the sycamore tree, I let my fingers slide over the smooth wood. Almost immediately, I was transported back in time to when I was a young boy roaming the hills and creek bottoms of this very farm.

It was a warm spring day. I was barefooted. Exploring the creek at the edge of the pasture far from home was my idea of a perfect day. That quickly changed when someone nearby hollered at me as I walked along a dusty cow path. Startled, I stopped and looked up to find a scary old woman standing thirty steps ahead in my path. She was known to our family simply as "Lou." Little was known about her except that she was a spinster who stayed by herself in a large rambling house at the edge of our property. She was rarely seen outside. Because of Lou's odd and superstitious ways, people in the community whispered among themselves about her. On that day, she was wearing a wide-brimmed straw hat and a black trench coat. Dingy white hair fell from under her hat, long and straight down to her waist. At my tender age, I thought she looked like the Wicked Witch in the Wizard of Oz. She carried a basket on one arm and walked with the aid of a crooked white stick. I froze in my tracks, scared stiff.

Lou, who was nearly deaf, screamed out to me in a scratchy, high-pitched voice, "Boy, you got the measles?" She shook her white walking stick at me and said, "I'm afeared of them measles; now git back."

I was in shock. I didn't know what to do. Finally, I found my voice and was able to answer, "No Ma'am. It's just my freckles." I wasn't sure she even heard me. She kept hollering something about picking poke salad greens and mushrooms. I shouted I had to go, then turned and ran straight to my house as fast as a rabbit.

I let Dad and Mother know about my encounter right when I got in the door. Of course, they knew Lou. I told them about her shaking her white walking stick at me and asking me if I had the measles. They calmed me down and let me know that Lou had a phobia about getting sick and that I would do well to give her plenty of room in the future. I didn't venture back to that part of the pasture for a long, long time.

I did see Lou one more time about a year later when she showed up at our back door. I hid in the bathroom while Mother went to talk to her. Then I heard Mother rustling around in the kitchen. I carefully peeked out the window and watched as Lou slowly walked away with a bag of food clutched in one hand and her crooked white walking stick in the other. That was the last time I saw Lou.

Now, as I held the white sycamore stick and relived that scary childhood experience with Lou, I realized that she had allowed her superstitions and worries to limit her world. She could not enjoy people or all the other gifts life had to offer.

I wrapped my fingers tighter around the white sycamore stick. Even though life can be treacherous and scary at times, I resolved right then and there to enjoy each day to the fullest and not let my own fears and worries control me. Glancing at my freckled hand, I thought of Lou; then I smiled and set off to enjoy the rest of my day.

The Sweetbay Tree / Photo by Benny Graves

# Chapter 8

## Go Skinny Dipping

I was in trouble again. Seems Mother had had enough of my pestering my three sisters just to hear them scream. I was a bored nine-year-old on a hot summer morning. I was sent outside to go play with Cousin Carl.

I raced across the road to meet up with my first cousin who was visiting for the week at Grandmother Graves's house. Carl was a tall, lean teenager, with jet-black hair and clear blue eyes. Everyone said he looked like a young Clint Eastwood who happened to be my TV hero at the time. Since he was five years older than me and lived far away, he was very cool. I idolized Carl.

That summer, I happily tagged along with him wherever he went. When he stopped, I bumped into him. The creek down in the pasture behind the barn was our favorite place to spend the day. This creek was a small, lazy stream with places you could jump across without getting your feet wet. In the bend of the creek where the water slowed down, pools would form deep enough to support some fish. Banks along the creek were high and steep where the water had gouged the earth deep during floods. In the hot days of summer, the water ran low and babbled through and around clumps of willow trees that grew there. Big shady oak trees with the occasional grape or muscadine vine draped from their limbs were scattered up and down the creek. In a strategic spot on the grass covered bank, an old sweetbay tree grew gracefully, its low hanging limbs filled with sweet-smelling blossoms. The creek was a perfect place for a couple of boys to escape on a summer's day.

To get to the creek from Grandmother's house, we had to walk down a long sloping hill, dodging cows gathered under shade trees. We especially kept a sharp eye out for that one mean red bull who might take a notion to chase you. But we always seemed to find a way to make it around these obstacles and arrive at the creek.

We spent hours playing. We waded up and down the creek bed in our ragged blue jean cutoffs collecting frogs, crawfish, and salamanders (mud puppies). Sometimes we chased minnows in the shallows with homemade nets made out of flour sacks, trying to capture them for fish bait. On the banks in the tall grass, we would catch green grasshoppers with our bare hands and put them in a glass Mason jar to add to our selection of fish bait. Carl would cut some river cane or a slender limb, and we would rig up fishing poles with lines and hooks we carried in empty matchboxes in our pockets. When the hooks were placed in the dark deep pools, we never knew what we might catch.

I remember catching red belly and goggle eye bream, maybe a small crappie or two. Occasionally, a small creek bass or a fat bullhead catfish would snag our bait and give us a fight. We even survived landing a stubborn snapping turtle once. He hissed through wide-open jaws, daring us to try to remove the hook. We decided to let him keep it and cut the line. As boys, we were naturally competitive and always kept count of who caught the most—or the biggest fish. Sometimes we would take some home on a stick stringer for Grandmother to cook for us.

When we weren't fishing, we might amuse ourselves by making stick boats and racing them down the swifter parts of the creek. The races were intense with lots of hollering, and they usually ended with one of us calling for a rematch. Sometimes we would even bring a watermelon from the family garden, lay it in the cool shallow water, and eat it later with our bare hands under the shade of the sweetbay tree.

Without a doubt, the best part of our time together on the creek was swimming at the "Swimming Hole." Within a stone's throw of that sweetbay tree was a wide, two-foot deep hole of water where the cows liked to drink. Their hooves had cut a deep v-shaped trail through the high banks down to the edge of the pool. This trail made a perfect runway for us to hit the water running full speed. After jumping into this shallow pool for a while, it did not take Carl long to figure out we needed to dam up the creek to deepen the water in our swimming hole.

We sneaked a shovel out of Dad's toolshed and grabbed an armload of empty burlap feed bags from the barn. Next we worked for hours shoveling sand and mud into bags and stacking them into a narrow cut in the creek bed. Then we shoveled dirt, hauled sand rocks, and placed them on top of the dam until Carl said it was right. We even constructed a burlap-covered spillway at one end of the dam for the water to overflow. The job we accomplished would have made the head engineer at the Army Corps of Engineers in Vicksburg proud. Water rose overnight, and the next day, we had a pool of water maybe four feet deep. Ten-foot tall banks served as our diving platform as we dove into the pool headfirst. My chest would sometimes scrape against the mud bottom. It was a miracle we survived without breaking our necks. We whooped and hollered, having a grand ole time in our improved swimming hole. We swam the day away until we heard Mother calling us to supper.

We were late getting to the swimming hole the next day because of some burdensome farm chores Dad gave us. After lunch, we were finally able to slip off to our fancy new pool. Racing past the old sweetbay tree, we both came to a screeching halt at the bank of the swimming hole. Three skinny black boys from some neighboring houses stood on the opposite bank. Obviously, they had come to swim. We stared at each other in silence across the creek for a minute, sizing up each other.

Before long, someone broke the ice and said, "It's hot out here. Let's go swimming."

You know, without any court orders, lawyers or politicians, we integrated the swimming hole down by the sweetbay tree on that summer's day back in 1964.

And swim we did. Our new friends stripped off all their clothes and hung them on some nearby bushes. Naturally, we took off our clothes too. Buck naked, we cannonballed in from our bank. They dove in from their bank, and we spent the afternoon generally showing out for each other. We found a grapevine and cut it at the ground to make a swing we used to launch ourselves over the water. We skinny-dipped for several hours that afternoon until Mother hollered for us to come. We said goodbye to our new friends, retrieved our clothes, dressed quickly behind the sweetbay tree, and left for our home on the hill.

A few days later, when we got to the swimming hole again, we found disaster had struck. The cows had tromped on our dam until the water had broken through and washed our hard work away. We were outraged at the cows. We slumped down on the edge of the bank in deep mourning. About that time, two of our new friends showed up to swim. After they saw the situation, they offered to help us build it back. Working together, we repaired the dam. By the next day, we had our swimming hole back.

It was great to get to know these new guys that summer. Friendships were made that remain to this day.

Down the hill from the barn, close to that long gone swimming hole, a large sweetbay still grows. It is a beautiful specimen with dark evergreen leaves that cast a wonderful shade. On this summer day, the tree is filled with small, sweet smelling, creamy white flowers, which look like miniature magnolia blossoms. The fragrant perfume of these blossoms triggers sweet memories of skinny dipping with my friends at the swimming hole.

Standing under this ageless tree, I think how simple life would be if people just relaxed and accepted others. That summer long ago, we all experienced a glimpse of true freedom.

The Christmas Tree / Photo by Benny Graves

# Chapter 9

## Be Generous

From somewhere deep within the dreams of a 10-year-old boy, I could vaguely hear my name being called over and over. Quietly, I pulled the warm patchwork quilt over my head and lay still as a mouse. The hum of our Hotpoint deep freeze at the head of my old metal bedframe sang me back to dreamland. My sleep was soon shattered by the booming voice of my Dad saying, "Boy, it's time to get up. It's Saturday, and we have work to do."

I put the pillow over my head and groaned. Mother gently pulled the covers back and said, "You better get up; your daddy needs you to go with him to find a Christmas tree."

With sleep no longer an option, I dragged myself from my bed and put my clothes on. I was not happy.

After a breakfast of hot buttered biscuits and homemade blackberry jelly, my attitude got better. It was a cold December morning, so I pulled on my big coat. The sun was just rising over the horizon above the pond as Dad and I left the house. As usual, we took care of the chores first. I counted the cows while Dad poured feed into the troughs. We both scattered some bales of hay out beyond the hickory tree for the hungry cows to devour.

When we finished, Dad asked me to get the axe out of the toolshed while he grabbed our old Homelite chainsaw. We placed the tools in the bed of our trusty International pickup, jumped in, and headed out. We traveled to the far side of the farm to a pasture across the main creek. On the way, Dad said we needed to cut some firewood and then search for a Christmas tree for Mother.

Dad drove the truck up beside a fallen oak tree on the creek bank. We got out and dropped the rusty tailgate. Dad sat down, gassed and oiled the chainsaw, and proceeded to pull on the starter rope a few times until it came to life in a cloud of blue smoke. Revving it up, he went to work on the treetop, cutting the limbs into perfect uniform sticks of firewood. My job was to throw the small limbs and all other scraps of wood onto a brush pile. After a couple of hours, he put down the saw, and we loaded the truck bed with a fine stack of firewood.

Sitting down on big blocks of wood, we took a break for a few minutes and enjoyed a Coke and a couple of leftover biscuits. Finally, Dad told me to hand him the axe. We took off to find our Christmas tree! Little did I know that this trip would change the way I thought about Christmas forever.

Walking together along the creek, we looked for a small well-shaped cedar tree that would make Santa Claus happy—and more importantly, please Mother. Running ahead through the broom sage, I spied a little group of cedars in a protected bend of the creek. When Dad caught up, we selected a six-foot tree with a good full shape and proceeded to chop it down. Dad selected another little cedar about four feet tall, gave me the axe, and told me to cut it too.

I asked him why we were getting two trees and he said, "You'll see."

Together, each of us grabbed a cedar tree and dragged them back to the truck. We loaded the trees, set the chainsaw on top of the firewood, and headed toward home.

As we got closer to home, Dad slowed down and turned off onto a rutted dirt road. This dead end road led to the home of an old widow woman who lived alone on the backside of our place. I couldn't figure out what we were doing. Dad said to just pay attention and do what I was told. We drove up to a run-down wooden shack. A couple of barking dogs rushed out from under the porch to announce our arrival. While I focused on the scraggly looking dogs through the truck window, Dad got out and stepped up on the porch and rapped on the screen door.

I could barely make out the figure of a stooped, grey-haired old woman peering out the door. They talked through the screen door a minute or two. As hard as I listened through the half-open truck window, I couldn't make out what they were saying. Dad came back and proceeded to back the truck up to the edge of the porch. He told me to hand him the smaller Christmas tree and to stack the firewood on the porch neatly against the wall by the door. With one eye on the two dogs sniffing the front tires of the truck, I slid out of the truck, quickly handed him the tree, and started to unload the firewood.

Dad disappeared behind the house and soon came back with an empty lard can. He stood the little cedar tree up in it and scooped some rocks and sand into the can from out of the driveway. He carried the tree into the house and came back out with the widow woman. They sat down in a couple of straight back wooden rockers on the porch and visited while I finished stacking the wood.

She mostly talked about her dear departed husband and how her family hardly came to see her anymore. When I finished my job , she stood up and said she'd be happy to pay Dad for the wood, but instead, he gave her a hug said it was a Christmas gift from our family. She was so grateful. She kept thanking us over and over. I thought I saw her wipe her eyes as we turned to leave.

With our one cedar Christmas tree still in the back of the truck, Dad cranked up the motor, waved goodbye to the widow woman, and left for home with the two dogs chasing alongside.   Riding along, Dad looked at me and gave me a pat of approval on my knee. He never said a word.

I have never forgotten that day and the powerful lesson I learned. That day, even as a young boy, I began to understand the true spirit of Christmas. Dad's actions clearly showed me that Christmas is a season of giving to others less fortunate.  The smell of fresh cedar each Christmas reminds me to be that generous person.

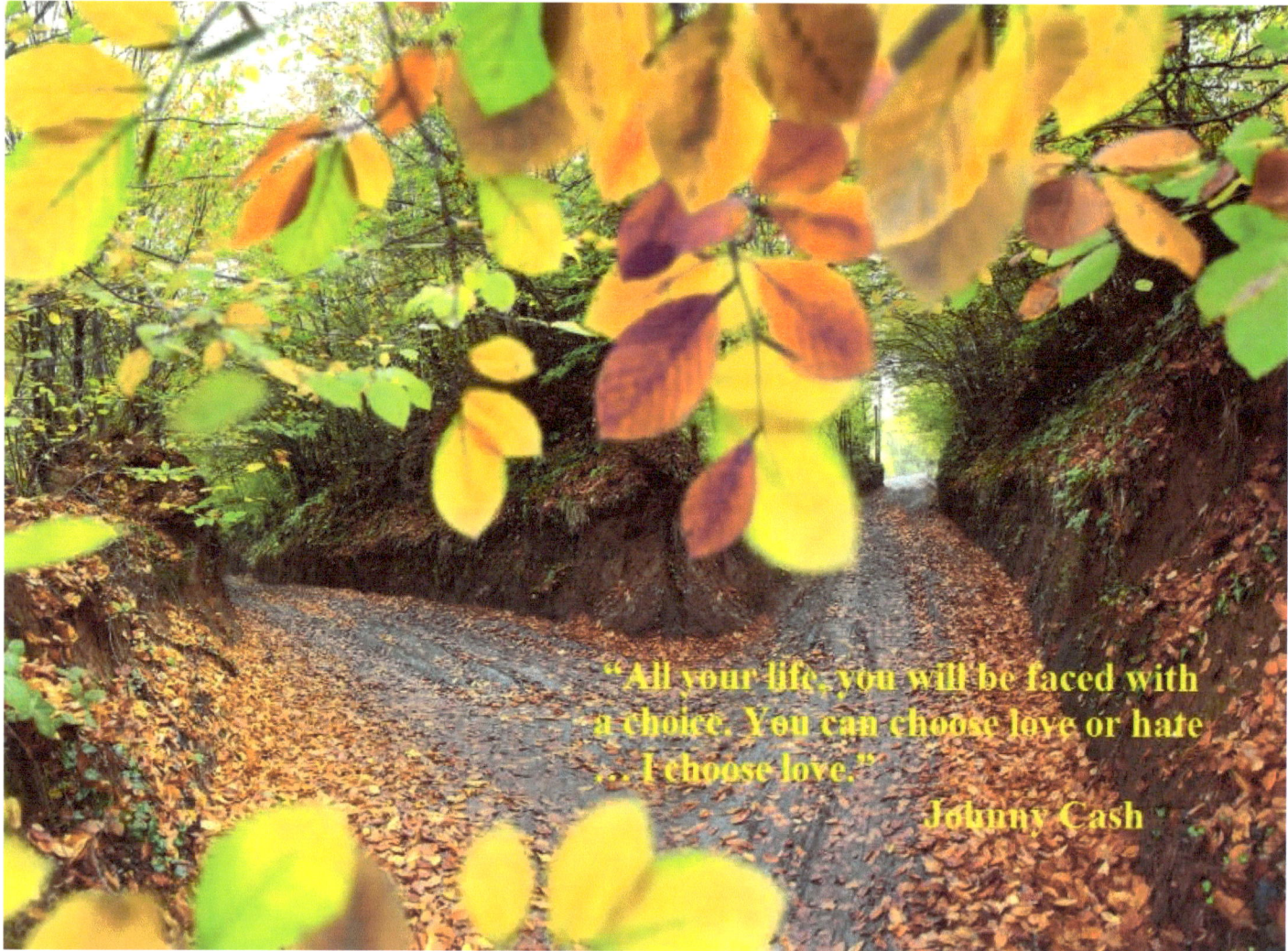

"All your life, you will be faced with a choice. You can choose love or hate …I choose love."

Johnny Cash

Photo by istock.com/bennygraves

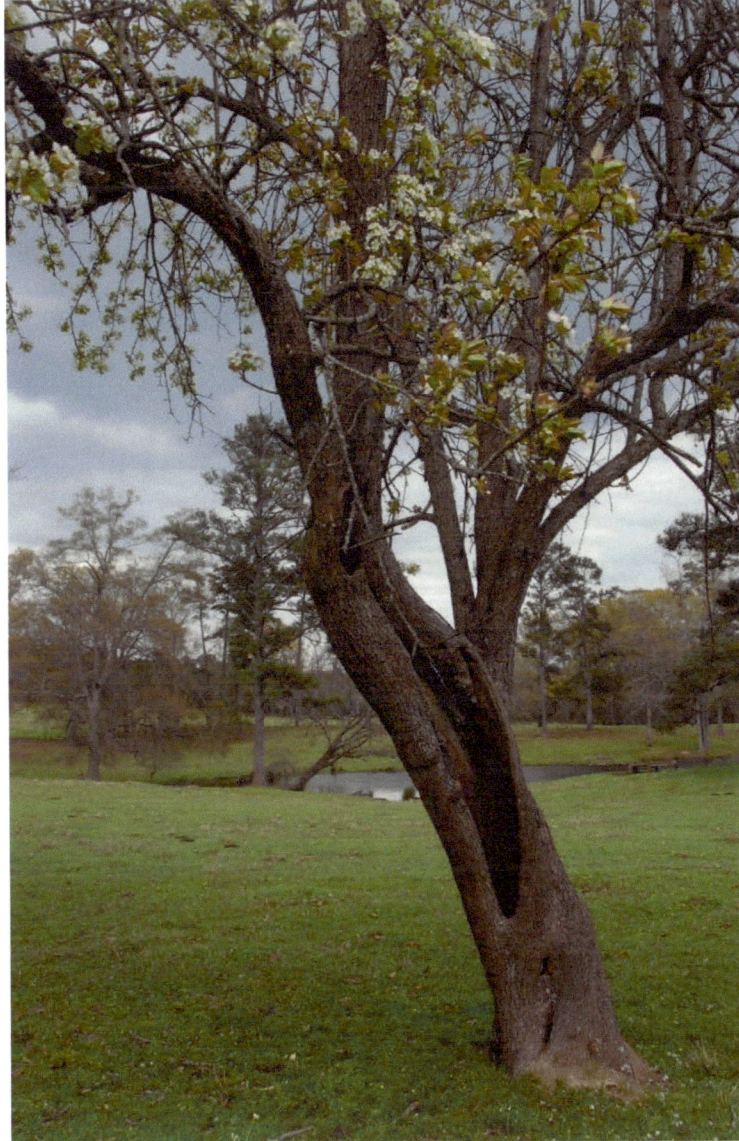

The Pear Tree / Photo by Benny Graves

# Chapter 10

# Be Determined

Hot biscuits right out of the oven, slathered with real butter and topped with a spoonful of homemade pear preserves. Ahh! The smell and the taste were incredible. I grew up on simple food served with love from my Mother's hand. The memory of this delicious Southern treat is etched in my mind forever.

The preserves were made from fresh pears picked from a single old tree that grew on the farm. Generations ago, one of my family members planted the tree, and even today, the gift of the pear tree continues. Although this tree is close to a hundred years old, it is still producing delicious, juicy pears. When you visit this unassuming tree, you immediately realize it is truly ancient. With a twisted, hollow trunk, growing at a seventy-degree angle from the earth, it is a picture of sheer determination. The bark on the lower half of the trunk is smooth from years of cows rubbing on it, urging the tree to drop just one more pear. It is truly amazing that the tree is still standing and bearing fruit.

In the earliest days of spring, the timeworn tree never fails to bloom. Tiny, delicate white blossoms blanket its branches like snow. What a delightful and welcome sight for all to see after a long drab winter. Wild honeybees appear as if on que, drawn to the short-lived bonanza of blossoms. Each little bee takes advantage of the early gift of nectar and pollen, savoring each blossom. After a short time, the flower petals silently fall, drifting down to carpet the ground in white, like a scene from a magical fairytale. Soon they vanish, gone in an instant.

A few days later, as I inspect the twigs closely, I see the tiniest of fruit already set and starting to grow. A wonder of nature, for sure. As the days of summer lengthen, the tree nurtures its crop of young, green pears.

In late August, the pears start to ripen, attracting all kinds of creatures during the days ahead. First the squirrels come while the weather is hot, trying to snag a juicy treat. Ever-present crows see the squirrels and soon struggle mightily to fly away with one of the golden globes in their beaks. Late in the evening, as the shadows grow long, you can catch a glimpse of an old doe and her two spotted fawns feeding on fruit left behind on the ground. After the momma deer gets a taste of the pears, she will return every day at the same time. You can set a watch by her routine. Early each morning, one old cow will leave the herd and come by the pear tree to search the ground for any fruit that may have fallen during the night. Watch closely and you will see as she stretches her neck up, straining her head high to reach toward the lowest branch. Then she'll extend her long tongue as far as she can to grip a leaf, then a twig, and at last, a pear. What a sight to witness.

With all of God's creatures competing to eat the ripening pears, my dear Mother would keep a close watch on the tree. When the pears were ripe enough, she would take us kids down to the tree to gather them. As a young boy, I would climb the leaning tree and shake the limbs until the pears rained down on the ground. Mother always told me to be careful and to hand pick some of the fruit to keep from bruising them. We all would have great fun filling a bucket or two with the greenish yellow treasure.

Later, back at the house, Mother, with the help of my sisters and our neighbor Inez, sat around the kitchen table peeling, coring, and slicing up the pears. My job was to carry the discarded peelings and cores out back of the house to feed a couple of hungry pigs in their fattening pen. I can still hear their squeals of delight when they saw me coming with that bucket.

In the kitchen, Mother would layer the fresh pear slices with sugar and let them sit for a while until there was plenty of sweet juice. Next, she slow cooked the juicy pears down until they transformed into a perfect, light golden amber. When the time was just right, and only she knew this from years of experience, she would fill hot

Mason jars with the sweet delicacy.  Jars would be sealed airtight, and their contents would be enjoyed all through the winter days ahead.  Mother's wonderful pear preserves have not been forgotten by anyone who ever sat at her table and tasted their goodness. Amen and pass the hot biscuits!

All of this enjoyment originated from just one old pear tree — a tree that continues to inspire my family with its determination to live and produce one more crop of fine pears.

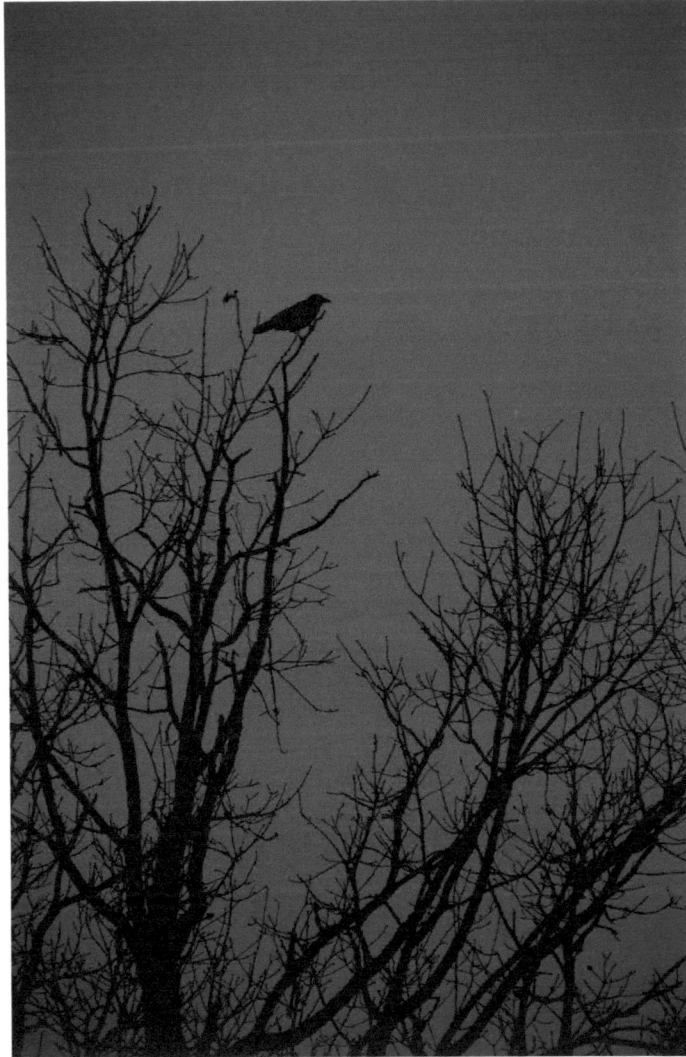
The Lookout Tree / Photo by Benny Graves

# Chapter 11

## The Rhythm of Life

The search is on as a barefoot boy and his Feist dog run quickly through the hallway of an old barn. Dark shadows of the musty smelling barn suddenly give way to the brilliant sunshine of a fresh summer day. The object of their search is still nowhere to be found. Spying a tall, slender post oak tree nearby, just right for climbing, the boy shinnies up the tree, leaving a concerned dog barking below. Like a sailor in a crow's nest on the mast of a tall sailing ship, the boy stands on a limb high in the tree, gripping the tree's main stem with one hand while he scans the fields below. The young lookout strains his eyes, intent on finding the one he seeks. Then, off in the distance, he finally spots him coming, walking slowly up the hill with a long handle hoe slung over his shoulder. The boy scrambles down the oak tree to the delight of the dog, and together, they run to meet Dad.

The Lookout Tree was always in the right place to view this ritual and all the other rhythms of farm life. Each day, Jersey cows walked up the nearby lane, passing under the post oak's shade to enter the barn, where they'd be milked twice a day, every day. Every summer, wagons stacked high with square bales of hay circled this tree as stout, bare chested young men tossed them over their heads into the loft of the big barn. For years, cattle on the farm have been fed daily in hand-made wooden troughs spread around the base of the post oak. The tree endured the trampling of countless hooves, which created knee deep mires of mud during cold wet winters and clouds of dust during hot, dry summer droughts. Yet the oak survived and flourished, giving real meaning to the phrase "post oak tough."

Yearling calves ready for sale were always caught in the rickety wooden corral that surrounded the tree. On one particular occasion, when I was still a teenager, Dad and I were in the corral sorting calves. Suddenly, without warning, a 400-pound bull calf broke from the rest of the herd and ran by the post oak tree in an attempt to escape.

Dad hollered above the bellowing herd, "Stop that calf, Son; don't let him get away!"

Being the strong young football player that I was, I instinctively tackled the yearling as he charged by. And the crazy ride began! Around and around the tree, the bull calf dragged me with clumps of mud and manure flying up in all directions. I had him around the neck, but I could not stop him.

In desperation, I bit hard into his ear. I think I got his attention because he immediately made straight for the board fence of the corral. Together, we hit the boards of the fence at full speed. Busted boards splintered and flew everywhere as I rolled free from the wild beast at last.

Now, I must say I had tackled all kinds of strong fellows on the football fields on Friday nights, but never, ever, had I tackled something with the speed and moves like this animal. When I finally came to, Dad was standing over me with a real concerned look on his face.

After spitting some hair out of my mouth, I said, with a sheepish grin, "Guess I let that booger get away, Dad, but at least I made him earn it."

The lookout tree was right there in the middle of it all. I suppose if the tree could have smiled, it would have.

Fifty years later, the same rugged post oak tree is much larger and anchors a new corral. The tree continues to serve as a silent witness to the comfortable rhythms of our farm life. Every day, cows are still fed, each summer hay is still cut, and in the fall, calves are still sorted for sale in the corral. This tree reminds me that life indeed has a rhythm, which fills me with a powerful sense of well-being and happiness. I find contentment with these routine seasonal farm activities that serve as a backdrop for my life.

As I step out the backdoor of the house to feed the cows on a cold gray winter's morning, I notice an old black crow as it lights in the very top of the old post oak. A jet-black silhouette standing alone on a slender bare branch, he surveys the fields below. He is the lookout now. I hear him "caw, caw, caw," calling to his family group feeding in the fields below.

The memory of another brave lookout years ago comes flooding back to me. I know exactly what the crow is seeing. Suddenly, a gust of cold wind blows through the branches, and I watch the old black crow as he spreads his wings and steps off his lofty perch into the wind. For a brief moment, he hovers in the wind, suspended between heaven and earth. Then with a slight tilt of his wings, he is lifted up, and he soars—and my heart soars with him.

The Tree That Saw It All / Photo by Benny Graves

# Chapter 12

## Respect

The gum tree saw it all.

An old abandoned sharecropper's house stands on the farm on a hill in sight of the pond. Known for generations simply as "Buster's House," the little house dates back as being at least a century old. It is the oldest original structure still standing on our family farm. Gone are the old mule barn, the corn crib, the smoke house, the huge sweet potato storage shed, and great grandfather's big house. Only Buster's House remains. A simple three room building measuring a meager 28 feet by 30 feet, the shack sits perched on foundation pillars fashioned from old sand stones and handmade bricks. Built by hand inside and out with wide solid pine boards sawn no doubt from some of the original trees on the farm. It is protected from the weather by a rusty roof made of tin, the old thick kind, made to last. A simple wooden front porch graces the entrance of the house. At the corner of the porch, a huge sweet gum tree grows, providing welcome shade through years of hot summers.

And the gum tree saw it all…

The old folks say that the house was home to a black family, headed by a tall, lanky man named Buster Robinson. He was known to all in the community as a hardworking, good man. He and his wife lived in this little house and raised nine children during some mighty hard times. How they made it work in this tiny house with nine children has always been a mystery to me. I can't imagine where they all slept.

Inside the house, a small brick fireplace framed by a simple black wooden mantle anchors the front room of Buster's house. A wood cook stove stood in the far corner of the back room. These were the only sources of heat during the cold nights of winter. I imagine the small third room was used for sleeping. In the heat of the summer, the family spilled out onto the front porch under the shade of the sweet gum tree growing nearby. Buster and his family did a lot of living in and around this old house.

In the nearby fields, Buster and his family raised cotton, corn, sweet potatoes, and watermelons using nothing but mules and plows and long handle hoes. They tended a large vegetable patch and raised pigs and chickens to feed an ever-growing family. Out back of their house, a few apple and Indian peach trees provided delicious fruit for the family to enjoy. Water was hauled in a bucket from a clear spring bubbling from the ground at the bottom of the hill. From the trees on the farm, Buster and his boys chopped firewood, split cedar fence posts, and hewed crossties for fifteen cents apiece to sell to the railroad. By the sweat of their brows, they worked the land for their food.

And the gum tree saw it all…

Sometime right after World War II, Buster's family scattered to seek something better in life. Whatever happened to Buster and his clan is one of those haunting unknown mysteries, lost with the passing of time. The abandoned shotgun house remained empty for years. Of course, things changed on the farm, too. Cotton and corn were no longer grown, and grandfather started a Grade A Jersey dairy. The land around Buster's House became pasture for the milk cows.

After grandfather's death, the farm shifted to raising beef cattle. From World War II until the early 60's, Buster's house sat vacant. In the peace and quiet, graceful barn swallows raised their broods each summer in sculpted mud nests tucked onto slender ceiling ledges under the porch.

And the gum tree saw it all…

I remember as a small boy discovering the old deserted shack on one of my many barefoot forays around the farm. I can still hear the sound of the weathered boards creaking as I stepped across the rickety old porch. The wooden front door was stiff and scraped across the floor as I shoved hard to open it. The smell of a stale old house hit me in the face as I slowly ventured into Buster's House for the first time.

As my eyes adjusted to the dim light, I could see an empty room with the simple small fireplace on the wall to my left.  Dusty cobwebs draped here and there across the room.   Globs of dirt dauber nests clung to the ceiling and walls in every nook and cranny. It was a spooky experience for a young boy trying his best to be brave.

Moving carefully into the back room in the dim light, I could see the old rusty metal cook stove in the corner and a wooden icebox nearby. A single board shelf hung on a wall with a few brown snuff bottles and two old empty coffee cans. Then, out of the corner of my eye, on the floor against the back wall, I spotted the long pale remains of a shed snake skin.

My nerve broke. It was time to go! I passed the trunk of the sweet gum tree in mid-air as I leapt off the edge of the porch and hit the ground running—running for home like only a scared little boy can.

And the gum tree saw it all…

As the beef cattle herd grew, my Dad started to use Buster's House to store hay. Every summer, Dad would trade with someone to cut and bale our hay. He would round up me and several local teenage boys to pick up and haul the square bales from the fields to our big barn. After we had completely filled the big barn's loft, we were tuckered out, but we still had to stuff Buster's House full of hay bales from floor to ceiling.

We would pull the wagons stacked high with hay as close to Buster's back door as possible. A couple of us skinny boys would slide through the narrow door of the rickety old house to take our turn stacking hay one bale at a time as it was thrown in the door. Of course the first poor guy in the shack usually got stung by some vicious red wasps. After much running and yelling and hurting and getting laughed at, we would finally settle down, kill the wasps, and unload the hay.

If you have never stacked hay bales in a sweaty, dark, dust-filled sharecropper's house in the middle of August in Mississippi, you have definitely missed a treat. Each young man was tested to his limit in front of his peers. This yearly ritual made men out of boys and taught us a work ethic that stuck with each of us for life.

Once the old house was filled with hay, we would collapse under the shade of the gum tree and celebrate with an ice cold Coca Cola brought to us by Mother. To this day, it remains the best drink I have ever tasted.

And the gum tree saw it all…

Over the years, Buster's House has faced all manner of storms and weather conditions: violent spring time thunderstorms with driving rain and strong winds, occasional winter snow drifting deep on a sagging roof, melting into a line of frozen daggers hanging from the edge of the tin roof. One particular storm in the summer of 2000 raked the farm with destructive straight-line winds. Many of the trees and buildings on the farm were ravaged. Roofs were peeled off, and timber was laid down by one huge sustained gust. In the hours after the storm, when I finally was able to make my way back to Buster's House, I was relieved to find it had survived the storm with only minor roof damage. The sweet gum tree, though missing one huge limb, was still standing guard as always at the corner of the house.

The tin roof was repaired, and the fallen limb was cut and removed. Some of the tin salvaged from other destroyed barns and outbuildings was used to cover the outer walls of Buster's House. The sheets of tin were screwed down tight onto the old weathered pine boards serving to strengthen and weather proof the little shack against future storms.

And the gum tree saw it all…

Large round bales have replaced the small square bales of hay once harvested from the fields. A new pole shed built a few feet from Buster's House now serves as hay storage. No longer needed to store hay, the house now serves as a storage unit for all manner of cast-off family belongings. Peering in the front door today, you would see a jumble of memories: childhood bicycles from that special Christmas long ago, a little red wagon too precious to throw away, an old worn ironing board, a wooden school desk—all little pieces of our fleeting lives. In the back room, salvaged planks of lumber are stacked out of the weather. Looping coils of rusty barbed wire lie piled in the corner. Loose straws of hay remain scattered all across the floor from days gone by.

Occasionally, through the years, I have gone to Buster's House to get a piece of lumber or to store some special item deemed too valuable to throw away. I did take notice that the old gum tree was growing even bigger. Its enormous branches stretched out above the roof as if embracing the aging house. But, I was busy and hurried quickly on.

And the gum tree saw it all.

Today, I tend to walk a little slower. After checking on a cow and her new calf the other day, I happened to walk by Buster's House. It was a crisp, clear autumn day. I felt somehow the old house was calling to me, and so I lingered. A sense of profound reverence flooded my heart; a respect for the house and for the lives it once protected hit me somewhere deep inside. I stepped around the corner of the house and sat down on the edge of the weathered front porch. Leaning back against a wooden post, I pondered Buster and his life on this piece of land, his wife and children, their joys and pain.

As I closed my eyes and relaxed in the sun, the sound of firewood being split with an axe came to me from somewhere behind the shack. The rhythm of each lick rang steady and strong. The sound of children laughing and playing drifted lightly in the air. It was a pleasing sound of pure innocent joy. Then, from inside, I clearly heard a mama's voice singing softly to her little baby. Boards creaking in time with the weight of a rocking chair as it tilted slowly back and forth, back and forth. Listening even closer, I became aware of a man moaning, moans of someone tired of the struggle, but too proud to give up. Was that Buster? I slowly opened my eyes and looked up to golden leaves shimmering in the sun. With a genuine respect for Buster and his House, I rose to go.

And this one old gum tree saw it all.

"To me a lush carpet of pine needles or spongy grass is more welcome
than the most luxurious Persian rug."
**Hellen Keller**

The Big Oak Tree / Photo by Benny Graves

# Chapter 13

## Treasured Memories

On an early June morning, already warmed by the summer sun, I find myself walking down the hill in the south pasture of the family farm. I arrive at the Big Oak tree and step into its cool shade. Magical shadows of lush green leaves dance at my feet and beg me to linger. I take a moment to sit down and lean against its ancient trunk. Almost immediately, my mind is transported back into folds of sweet memories. I think of the men of my family who came before me, my dad and my grandfather, each in his own time enjoying the shade of this very same tree. Both men are gone now but not forgotten.

Standing alone on an old fence line, this massive willow oak dominates the landscape in every direction. The tree's beauty is simply breathtaking to behold. When you come into its presence, it demands your full attention, your awe, a measure of reverence. The trunk, with a girth of seventeen feet, is covered with beautiful dark gray bark, which seems to flow straight down from high above to flare out at the last minute over a mighty base just before touching the earth. Roots unseen spread out deep and wide to firmly anchor the regal giant. To appreciate its height, it causes you to tilt your head back, way back, til' your neck hurts. In stunned silence, you see it tower, ever upward to finally touch the blue of the summer sky. Huge limbs stretch out in all directions forming the arches of a perfect living cathedral. Of all the trees on the farm, the Big Oak is the uncontested king.

Grandfather purchased the land where the Big Oak reins in 1920 for fifty cents an acre. He moved to this parcel of land to till the soil and to nurture his growing family. Family history says he worked side by side with several black men with solid names like Titus, Dave, Isaiah, and Pink. Together, they used crosscut saws, axes, and fire to clear the virgin trees from the land. Fires burned day and night for weeks at a time. Sweat flowed from both men and beasts day after day. I can only imagine the relentless toil. Finally, the new ground was ready to be plowed with teams of mules. Crops of cotton, corn, watermelon, and sweet potatoes were planted and harvested with the rhythm of the seasons. One by one, all the trees covering the fields were sacrificed to make room for the plow.

Only one fortunate tree was spared: a willow oak. You see, men working the fields during this era always left one good tree. When you work the fields in the hot summer sun, you need a shade tree for mules and men alike to rest beneath. This one lone oak provided this cool sanctuary. The thought of my grandfather resting his mules under this very same oak means more to me than words can express.

Six days a week, grandfather worked hard, but on Sunday, he rested. Grandmother used to tell me how she and grandfather would walk hand in hand across the fields on pleasant Sunday mornings, taking a short cut to attend church. The path took them down a sloping hill behind their house, under the Big Oak, and through the fields of growing crops. After crossing a little creek on a line of stepping stones, they would then walk to the top of the next hill, to arrive at their church.

The Big Oak was a silent witness to my grandparents' faithfulness to worship God. They were simple people who taught their children and grandchildren to trust in God and to always do the right thing in life. Today, that same oak tree quietly reminds me of this powerful lesson.

In his later years, Grandfather transitioned the row crop farm into a fine little Grade A dairy. His three sons delivered whole milk in classic glass milk bottles to customers all around our town and the surrounding countryside. Running the dairy was hard work for the whole family during those years.

Unfortunately, while herding a Jersey cow with a new baby calf at her side, my grandfather suddenly fell to the ground, dead of a massive heart attack. He was seventy-six years old. They found him just a few hundred feet from the Big Oak. Somehow, it comforts me to know this special tree witnessed the passing of my beloved grandfather.

My father, as the oldest son, immediately took over the family farm. Over time, he changed the farm to a small beef cattle operation and also worked full time at a nearby University. On Saturdays, in the heat of summer, you could always find him wearing his long sleeved khaki coveralls while bush hogging the old fields and pastures.

One of my favorite memories as a young boy is of taking my father a drink of water in a Mason jar. As I sit under the oak tree now, I can clearly see this ritual as if it were yesterday—Dad stopping his old pop John Deere tractor under the shade of the Big Oak as I hurried barefoot down a dusty cow path to hand him a cool drink.

He would always say, "That tastes mighty good, Son."

I would give anything to hand Dad just one more cool drink of water under the shade of the Big Oak tree.

On this hot summer day, as I lean against the rough bark of the Big Oak tree, I feel the wonderful presence of my Dad and my Grandfather. Treasured memories float to me on the breeze, and just for a moment, the cool shade of the Big Oak covers us all.

Climb a tree – it gets you closer to heaven.

**Author Unknown**

The Lone Oak / Photo by Benny Graves

# Chapter 14

## Loneliness

Dark and massive, a rugged trunk tilts with a slight lean earned from years of endurance. It is a huge Southern red oak, rooted deep in the land. From all sides, enormous spreading limbs grow thicker than a man, stretching far out and up to embrace the sky. Strong, partially exposed roots run out from the base in every direction like the gnarled fingers of an old woman clutching the earth. On a hill, it stands alone— a picture of loneliness.

For over six decades, I have lived within sight of this old tree. Yet, each time I take the time to look it over, another little piece of its rich character is revealed—things like the small opening at its base, which serves as an entrance to a mysterious, dark hollow cavity—the dimensions of which only the wild creatures know.

I have witnessed its tiny, delicate flower catkins on an early spring morning, showering clouds of pollen into the gentle breeze. Limbs, long and twisting, randomly branch upward and outward into innumerable twigs filled with green leaves of summer—each one reaching out, searching for that perfect spot to bask in the sun. In winter, I have observed the numerous small round galls, which populate its bare branches. They serve as evidence of the tree's relationship with tiny specialized wasps who have laid their eggs to be nurtured by the tree.

With my hands, I have touched its rough gnarled roots, which spread out across the ground before plunging into the dirt. They serve as the perfect anchor for this huge lone oak. This tree with all its unique charms somehow connects with me.

This lone oak, like so many old oaks on farms across the South, marks the location of a home place from long ago. My family history says this very tree anchored the front yard of my great grandparents' house. It was a grand two story house with porches wrapped all the way around both levels. On the bottom floor, two dogtrot hallways split the house in both directions. Eight brick fireplaces graced this elegant wood-framed home. It was one of the nicest houses in the community during its time.

They say a mysterious fire took the house to the ground on a cold winter's night in the year before World War II. Family members escaped the fire, and the house was never rebuilt. Somehow the oak survived this catastrophic event.

Today, this single tree is all that marks the spot where the grand old house once stood. As the cold wind of winter whistles through its bare branches, one old Southern red oak stands alone to watch over all that used to be.

But then, in the spring, when the new grass of April grows, the cows bring their new calves around to lie down together under the shade of this lone oak tree. I notice the wild flowers blooming all around the tree in random beauty. From the branches above, I hear the cooing of a morning dove as she calls to her mate. A perfect picture of peace and harmony settles upon the land. My eyes soak in the peaceful scene, and my heart smiles… for now I finally understand a secret truth about the tree: the lone oak is not really alone.

"When a man plants a tree, he plants himself."
**John Muir**

The Twice Struck Tree / Photo by Benny Graves

# Chapter 15

## Perseverance

For those who say lightning never strikes the same place twice, I simply direct them to check out a big, tall Loblolly pine tree growing above the watershed lake on the farm. Two wide scars run down its trunk. Two different storms, years apart, hurled lightning bolts directly upon this unfortunate tree. Of all the hundreds of trees scattered across our property, what are the odds that a lightning bolt would touch this one tree not once but twice?

While out searching for a lost calf, I noticed the first wound a few days after a particularly intense spring thunderstorm had passed. A nasty streak of missing bark as wide as my hand was peeled in a perfect corkscrew fashion down and around the massive pine's trunk. My heart sank, for as all Southern country folks know, lightning strikes are a death sentence to a pine tree. If the strike itself doesn't kill the tree outright, then the pine beetles move in, attracted to the smell of a wounded tree, finishing it off with a slow, sure death.

I watched during the first few months for the tell-tale signs of decline. I even thought how I would have to borrow a bigger chainsaw to fall this tree when it finally died. But, a year or so later, I was amazed to observe that the tall pine was surviving. Over several more years, the gaping wound slowly healed to leave only a ragged scar. I was so happy for the tree.

Then Ka-Boom! In a flash, the same giant pine took another direct hit from a lightning bolt thrown from a black August thundercloud. I could not believe the bad luck this tree had experienced to be struck a second time.

A fresh streak of bark was blown away straight down one side of the trunk. There it stood oozing resin, wounded again. What a sad sight.

In the next few months, I just knew this mighty pine would succumb to what nature had dealt out in its never-ending cycle of life and death. I waited and watched the wounded tree for signs of browning needles in the crown or for the pitch tubes of active beetles feeding along the injured trunk.

Again, over time, I was astounded to see the tall pine live through this second brush with certain death. How this specimen survived these two grievous wounds and now thrives is beyond my understanding. What a victory for one incredible tree. It is something worthy of celebration.

The stately old pine, with its two old scars, still grows today on that little rise of ground above the lake. This special tree teaches me that life can triumph over tragedy. It is even possible to experience multiple catastrophic life events and survive—even thrive.

These days, I don't give up quite as quickly because I know that, despite the odds being stacked against me, with perseverance and time, I can overcome misfortune. The lesson has been learned, transferred from a magnificent tree to a simple man. Today and every day, I celebrate the lesson of the twice struck pine.

Photo by istock.com/bennygraves

"In nature, nothing is perfect. Trees can be contorted, bent in weird ways
and they're still beautiful."
**Alice Walker**

The Inez Pine / Photo by Benny Graves

# Chapter 16

## Enduring Friendship

In a secluded corner close to the back property line of the farm, across a little spring-fed creek, a mammoth Loblolly pine tree grows. This huge tree represents the last vestige of virgin forest, which once covered the land. Through the years of its life, it has weathered all of nature's fiercest storms. More than that, this fortunate pine has survived generations of men clearing the land. Today, it stands proudly as a living testament to endurance.

It is as if I am entering a long forgotten sanctuary as I step into the little grove where this majestic pine resides. I pass by several trees—all kinds, both great and small. Then suddenly, there it is, in all its regal glory. Stepping up close to the tree, you are struck by its huge thick trunk, protected by thick scales of bark covered with the moss and lichen of old age. Straight and tall, the tree dwarfs all the other nearby trees.

Even though I crane my neck back to look upward into the crown, I never quite see the very top. But I know the blue sky surely begins where the last needle of this ageless tree ends. Sitting down at the base of this old giant on a thick brown carpet of pine needles this crisp autumn day, I feel the tree full against my back, smell its pungent scent of pine in the air, and hear the faint whisper of wind high above as it plays among the green tipped branches. It seems as if time has been suspended creating an enchanting experience. In this moment of quiet solitude in nature's sanctuary, I contemplate all things dear.

Standing as it does on the back edge of the farm's property line, this old pine looks over the home of Inez, one of our family's dearest friends. Inez is an elderly black lady, widowed for many years, with no surviving children. For years, she lived back off the road in a small, red-brick house in sight of this old pine. Like the tree, Inez stands tall and straight and proud. In her nineties now, she too has stood the test of time. Her endurance speaks for itself.

Inez is one of those special people who spreads the gift of laughter and lively fun with whomever she meets. Over the years, Inez has worked long hours right alongside our family, tending a large vegetable garden. I treasure the times she spent with us shelling purple hull peas or shucking sweet corn under the shade trees behind our house. Hilarious stories and sayings that she shared still ring in my ears. Oh, how we laughed! With Inez around, work was a pleasure, and time flew.

Some folks in the community might have thought she was a little eccentric and odd. Maybe so, but I knew there was a heart of gold beating inside her.

Through the years, Inez loved to go fishing. She had trod a well-worn footpath leading from her back doorstep, under the fence by the old pine, and across our pasture to the farm pond. After she sat down on her five-gallon bucket, she'd get a dip of Sweet Garrett snuff, pick up her long cane pole, and fish. She was always hoping to snag that one big catfish known to prowl the depths of the water. Occasionally, I would come by, sit on the grass beside her, and listen to her fun stories and serious bits of wisdom gleaned from a lifetime of living. Those were some rich times for me and served to deepen our friendship.

Long after they stopped gardening, she was faithful to visit Mother and Dad as they aged and became homebound. Each day, for years, she bounced in the door to check on them and to spread her cheer. She later sat with me on the family church pew at each of their funerals. She taught me by example what true friendship is.

Inez is in her twilight years now. Broken health of old age has resulted in her moving to a distant care facility. Our family visits her as often as we can. Her eyes still sparkle up at us as we lean over her hospital bed.

Thankfully, her fun spirit is not broken, evidenced by her bright purple painted fingernails she proudly showed us during one of our last visits.  Our family's special bond of love with Inez will never end.

In a secluded back corner of the family farm, the old pine stands tall, proud and true, faithfully watching over Inez's empty house. The other day, as I approached the old pine, I noticed a faint overgrown footpath running right beside the tree, under the barbed wire fence, and directly to the back doorstep of Inez's house.  As I sat down and leaned back against the broad solid tree, my mind immediately thought of my dear friend Inez.

In the quietness, something spoke to me very clearly, piercing straight to my heart. From now on, the regal old pine would forever be known as the "The Inez Pine."

The Holly Tree / Photo by Benny Graves

# Chapter 17

## Family Tradition

Out in the edge of our farm's main hay field, a beautiful mature American Holly tree grows. A large, multi-trunk specimen, it is topped with layer upon layer of glossy green leaves, decorated each winter with an abundance of bright red berries. This striking tree has earned our admiration through the years by playing a part in a family tradition for generations.

In spring, the holly tree blooms with a profusion of the tiniest of white flowers, scattered like drops of dew among its leaves. Wild honeybees from miles around collect its nectar and pollen. Sometimes on a warm spring day, I stand quietly under the tree, with my eyes closed and listen to the drone of happy bees above. The sound is sublime.

Later, in the early days of summer, the nest of a mockingbird can be found in one of the lower branches nestled among the green barbs of holly leaves. If I dare to peek into the nest, I will experience the swift wrath of a mama bird protecting her young. Like a screaming miniature dive-bomber, she swoops down at my head again and again until I make a hasty escape. Then, in triumph, she returns to the tip-top of the tree to declare her victory to the world.

I'm always careful in the late summer not to injure the holly tree when mowing hay. Removing the tree entirely would make haying so much easier. Instead, each year, I'm faithful to protect this beautiful little tree and allow it to continue to grow freely where it stands because it means too much.

On crisp, fall evenings, as the sun begins to set, I notice sleek, white-tailed deer as they quietly slip from the adjoining woods into the hay field to nibble on tender red clover. They seem to always meander toward the holly tree. Its low spreading limbs give them a sense of security and a place to mark their territory.

When the white frost of winter blankets the ground, I have seen a majestic buck deer standing alert under the green and red boughs of the tree, framed for a fleeting moment like a picturesque Hallmark Christmas card — a classic scene captured forever in the camera of my mind.

As Christmas Day approaches, the holly tree is at its peak of glory, decked out with shiny green leaves and brilliant red berries. It is a natural beauty standing out against the drab grey landscape of winter. One of my earliest memories of growing up on the farm is Mother holding my hand and walking with me and my sisters across the hay field to collect a basket full of holly twigs with berries to be used as holiday decorations around the house.

In fact, every year, this special tree has presented our family with fresh yuletide trimmings. Countless Christmas wreaths and garlands have graced our home, providing the perfect festive touch of nature's green.

When my wife and I moved back to the family farm, we always made a point of walking with our two little girls and Sunny, our golden retriever, down to the holly tree each Christmas season. On the way, we would throw a few sticks for Sunny to retrieve and have a grand time collecting holiday greenery and making sweet memories. Our girls grew up enjoying the gifts of the holly tree, too.

Time continues to slip on by, stopping for no one. Mother and Dad have passed on. Their bodies now rest in the community cemetery on a neighboring hill within sight of the farm. The sisters have all married and moved to other states. My grown daughters have busy careers. Occasionally, Christmas draws all of us back to the home place — back together as family to eat and laugh and love and to walk once again down to the old holly tree—to a tree that has given us much more than Christmas twigs full of red berries. It has given us a cherished family tradition.

I Hear the Acorns Fall / Photo by Benny Graves

# Chapter 18

## Nature's Unending Cycle of Life

As dawn breaks in the eastern sky, I leave the house and strike out to walk alone among the oaks. Cool damp autumn air greets me as I glide quietly through a misty ground fog suspended under old familiar trees. With chilled hands shoved deep inside the pockets of my faded jeans, I stop and lean against the trunk of a massive white oak to watch the sun rise in all its glory. In the distance, the first crow calls loudly announcing the new day. A squirrel barks a feisty reply. Close by, little birds of all descriptions start their chirping and flit about as the forest begins to wake up and come alive.

Suddenly with the faintest stirring of a breeze, I hear the steady plop, plop of acorns falling. Like heavy drops of rain, they tumble from a colored canopy high above, landing all about me near and far—each one answering Earth's call with perfect timing to rest on ancient ground—a gift showered from above to all of us creatures below. Bowing low, I acknowledge the gift by scooping up three shiny brown acorns. Placing them deep in warm pockets, I watch the sunbeams chase the shadows across the forest floor.

A few feet from the big oak, I notice a young oak sapling standing three feet tall. It serves as evidence that one acorn beat the odds of being eaten by hungry wildlife. One fortunate little tree waits at its mother's feet for its turn to grow toward the sun.

After a few minutes, I leave for home. Meandering slowly back through the oaks, I contemplate nature's unending cycle of life all around me. A light wind again rustles through the leaves above, and like rain, I hear the acorns fall. I smile to myself as I savor the magic of it all.

Photo by istock.com/bennygraves

"Mockingbirds don't do one thing but make music for us to enjoy. They don't eat up people's gardens, don't nest in corncribs, they don't do one thing but sing their hearts out for us. That's why it's a sin to kill a mockingbird."

Harper Lee, *To Kill a Mockingbird*

Out of Destruction / Photo by Benny Graves

# Chapter 19

## Hope

The NOAA meteorologist said it was a "Derecho." Heck, I didn't even know what that was. I only knew that out of nowhere, a huge windstorm blew across the farm late one August afternoon, causing severe, widespread damage. In one fell swoop, numerous mature trees were uprooted and laid to the ground. Tin roofs from barns and outbuildings were ripped off in sheets and tossed across the entire landscape. For days, tin was found wrapped like aluminum foil around random tree trunks, fence posts, or whatever stood in their way.  In short, it was a mess of epic proportions.

When I could finally get to the scene a couple of hours after the storm, I couldn't believe the destruction. After hugging my family and finding everyone okay, I started picking my way through the damage around the farm. I found fences flattened in every direction by massive fallen trees.  Cows had to be rounded up and penned in secure corrals until emergency repairs could be made. In certain areas, dozens of huge pines had been blown to the ground, all lying in the same direction like giant toothpicks. Their root balls jutted up in the air with wet red mud, the color of blood still dripping off their exposed roots. It was a surreal, grotesque scene unfolding before me as I walked farther and farther across the farm.   I still remember the sick feeling in the pit of my stomach as I fully realized the scope of the disaster.

Instinctively, I grabbed my big chainsaw and started cutting big fallen trees off the perimeter fence line. It didn't take long in the August heat for me to feel overwhelmed with exhaustion. Sitting on a log, my clothes soaked in sweat, I realized my one chainsaw was no match for the enormous job ahead. As the sun set, I knew I would need lots of help and heavy equipment to clean up the downed trees and put all the buildings and fences back in order.

As darkness fell, I climbed into my pickup truck and slowly drove toward home. On the drive back, it started to sink in that this enormous clean-up operation was going to take a long time. I found myself sitting in the driveway in a numb trance, not knowing what to do next. For me, it was a very low, humbling moment in my life. I turned the key off and went inside.

That night, almost immediately, I started getting calls and visits from family and friends wanting to know what they could do to help. Cousins Carl and Rodney, who lived an hour away, heard of my predicament and volunteered to stop what they were doing and bring their logging trucks and equipment over. This was especially good news, for I soon learned that all the local logging crews were already swamped with similar emergency salvage requests. It was a great day when my cousins rolled through the farm gate with their heavy logging equipment in tow.

With their assistance, over the next few weeks, we were able to salvage several loads of logs from the storm-damaged timber. Later, another friend brought his bulldozer and pushed up the tops and root balls into burn piles. Another friend and his work crew came to repair the damaged farm buildings.

Over the next year, all buildings were repaired or reroofed, except for one. Sadly, the old original big barn, built by my grandfather in the early 1920's, was too far gone and was pushed up in a jumbled pile of lumber and later burned. Many memories went up with those flames.

Family helping family and friends helping friends pulled me through this life-changing event. I am forever grateful to all who pitched in to clean up the farm. The restoring power of these people who cared enough to help when I was down is a life experience I will never forget.

Two years later, I was rebuilding a storm-damaged fence line when I noticed a small water oak seedling sprouting from the top of a root ball of a huge pine tree blown over by the windstorm. This one little tree pushing up in the midst of all the destruction around it somehow touched me. Hope was alive! I made sure not to disturb the little tree perched high on that leftover red clay root ball.

I've watched this tree for years now, and I am impressed at its tenacity and will to survive, under difficult circumstances. It continues to grow into a beautifully shaped young oak. This tree serves as a reminder to me that although nature can destroy, it also restores itself with new life. One young tree representing hope born out of destruction. I am blessed to watch it grow.

The Leaning Tree / Photo by Benny Graves

# Chapter 20

## Appreciate the Simple Things of Life

On top of a hill overlooking the farm pond, four handmade feed troughs are stationed. Early each morning, eighteen black cows meet me there. From the bucket I carry, I pour a blend of cottonseed meal and corn into each wooden trough. As the jostling cows begin to eat, I look over each animal, making sure they are all present and okay. Through this time honored daily routine, we have grown to know each other quite well.

While the cows enjoy their morning feeding, I usually step back, pause and gaze down toward the edge of the pond. An odd slippery elm tree grows there. Unlike normal trees, this elm tilts at a most unnatural 45-degree angle with its trunk and crown stretching far out over the water. Although well rooted on the bank's edge, I wonder how it remains in such a precarious position year after year. This unique tree is one of my favorites on our family farm.

Every morning, this charming tree dares the boy within me to scramble out onto its outstretched trunk, to sit down and dangle my toes above the water. How nice it would be to skip work, relax, and daydream the day away.

As I come and go each day, this iconic elm is an endless source of wonder. Watching it change with the seasons is a pure, simple joy. For instance, in the early spring, it is one of the first trees to green up. Little buds swell and burst forth with fresh tidbits of green. The awakening of this tree is a sure signal that the cold dreary days of winter are finally coming to an end and will be soon replaced by the warmer days of spring. By late May,

I see lush, dark green leaves hanging low, casting their collective shade on the water below. Fat bream swirl to make their beds in the shallow water beneath the leaning trunk. At sunrise, on a hot summer morning, across the pond, I see a timid doe slip down to the water's edge for a cool drink. From above, a lone kingfisher dives for its breakfast, returning to the top branch of the elm with a squirming minnow held tight in its beak.

With the first frosts of autumn, I watch as the green leaves slowly transform into a cloud of vibrant yellow. Then, one perfectly still morning, as shafts of light shine down from a rising sun, the reflection of the leaning tree is mirrored in the dark tranquil pond, while random yellow leaves release themselves, one by one, drifting slowly down to kiss the water in silence... a breathtaking scene. As the last leaf lets go, bare branches prepare for the deep sleep of winter. Soon cold wind blows against my face as I make my daily visit to feed the hungry cows on the hill.

One day, without warning, a rare Southern snow makes its appearance with big feathery flakes floating quietly down from heavy grey clouds. Oh, what a wonderland! The snow soon paints the leaning tree into a perfect picture of contrast. Pure white powder draped against the dark grey bark of the trunk progresses up through the branches all the way to the tips of the twigs. A marvelous winter scene is frozen forever in the photographs of my mind.

This unusual tree, which has captured my daily attention for years, continues to provide me great pleasure. The leaning tree has taught me to slow down and enjoy the simple things of life. It reminds me to observe the little things of nature and to appreciate them for what they are... true gifts from God—gifts money can never buy.

In the early morning dew, I start down the path to feed the cows on a hill above the pond. I can't wait to see my longtime friend ... The Leaning Tree.

The Sassafras Grove / Photo by Benny Graves

# Chapter 21

## Dream

Some dreams do come true.

Out the backdoor of my childhood home past Buster's house in the midst of a little piece of bottomland, a spring fed creek flows. When I follow the creek upstream, I come upon one of the most magical spots on our farm. In a small cove among lush green ferns, a natural spring of cool, clear water flows from a tall sandy bank. Ageless wild azaleas and a single dogwood tree flank the bubbling spring. Tall oak trees rise above it all and lend their shade to this pristine southern landscape. As I approach, I am greeted by a grove of slender tall sassafras trees scattered along the bank in front of the spring. The ground beneath these trees is carpeted with soft, green moss begging to be touched.

It was here, as a teenager surrounded by the serene splendor of nature, I sat and dreamed the dreams of a young man. In these daydreams, I would meet the perfect girl with skin softer than the reindeer moss at my fingertips. Of course, I dreamed of being free of my parents… just me and that girl with the soft skin. In my dreams, we would go hand in hand to discover the world beyond the farm. Together, we would share the adventure of life at full speed.

I would be awakened from my dreams by the sound of birds singing among the sassafras leaves. Their songs sung against a backdrop of running spring water served to softly bring me back to the real world… or was this real?  I loved to come, sit by the spring and dream.

One day, I told my grandmother about the sassafras trees beside the spring. Right away, she asked me to bring her a handful of sassafras roots so she could brew us a pot of tea. She gave me instructions to smell the roots I dug up. She said I would know which ones were sassafras by their strong odor. Off I went, down to the spring, with a shovel in my hand. I dug up several small roots under the trees and cut into them with my pocketknife. As instructed, I smelled each one. Their strong licorice scent told me I had the real thing.

Back at Grandmother's house, the roots were washed and trimmed and covered with water. She brewed up a light colored mixture in a pot on the kitchen stove. I will always remember sipping my first cup of hot sassafras tea on the back porch with Grandmother. She told me the old folks often used it as a spring tonic. According to her, sassafras tea would cure what ailed you. My young immature palate quickly decided all I needed was a tiny sip of this strange brew! But what a grand time we shared.

Visiting the gurgling spring in the fall was always a colorful event. After the first Jack Frost touched the land, the grove of sassafras trees always put on a spectacular show. Their leaves changed into a cloud of vibrant yellow and crimson shimmering against a deep blue autumn sky. It was easy for me to lie down on the moss-covered ground at their feet, listen to the breeze rustle through the leaves above, and let it take me away to dreamland. In my dreams, I could do anything. I was strong and ran like lightning on the football field on Friday nights. Our team won game after game. The cutest cheerleader always rewarded me with a kiss as I walked off the field when the final horn sounded. I celebrated with my teammates and friends after each game. We were forever young. Nothing was impossible. It was great to dream.

Falling leaves tickled my face and wakened me from my bliss. I would step down to the spring for a drink of cold water. Using nothing but my hand as a cup, I drank my fill of pure spring water. It was always difficult to leave this place. Lightly stepping up out of the oasis, I walked through the grove of brightly colored sassafras trees and headed back home.

Later in my mid-twenties, I met a dark haired girl. In a short time, I was smitten. I brought her home with me one spring day to meet my parents. As young couples do, we excused ourselves after eating Mother's big meal and took a walk around the farm. I wanted to share my magical spot with her along the little creek. Soon we strolled through the grove of sassafras trees, and the spring came into view. It was as if we were entering our own private Garden of Eden. To one side, the dogwood tree stood dressed in white. Beside the water, wild azaleas bloomed with layers of delicate, pink flowers cascading down to the water's edge. Violets of lavender bloomed here and there among the brown leaves on the surrounding bank. At the back of the cove, clear spring water trickled from the earth into this idyllic setting.

My special girl fell in love with my spring fed sanctuary. In her excitement she grabbed my hands and we danced together among the sassafras trees. Throwing our heads back with laughter, we watched the budding leaves and branches whirling above in a kaleidoscope of blue and green. Finally, out of breath, we sat down side by side on the moss-covered bank, just me and that girl with the soft skin. All I can say is some dreams do come true.

Take time to dream.

The Cherry Pie Tree / Photo by Benny Graves

# Chapter 22

## Surprises

The best pie I never ate came from a cherry tree and was baked by my sweet bride. That pie taught me a great lesson about marriage.

We were newlyweds making a home in the old farmhouse where my grandparents had once lived. We didn't have a lot, but our love was strong. Because we had dated for several years, we thought we knew a lot about each other. However, living together for the first time, we were learning new things at warp speed—things we hadn't known at all about each other. We were making adjustments daily on the fly, determined to make our marriage the best ever. Like all couples, a few surprises came along.

My young wife put a lot of effort into learning which foods I liked to eat. She wanted to please me and worked hard to improve her cooking skills. She loved trying new things, and I loved to eat. I had no problem being her guinea pig. She watched my face closely as I ate and took notes on her recipe cards.

We had a special little cherry tree on our farm that had been planted years ago. Dad had ordered it from a fruit tree nursery after tasting some fresh cherries on a tour up north. It produced tangy flavored fruit, which made the best pies. The first summer after we married, it was loaded with a bumper crop of fat red cherries. One day I casually remarked that I loved cherry pie. Little did I know what lay ahead.

I arrived home from work the next day, and we sat down for supper at our special kitchen table made for two. It was only 2x3 foot, which meant we were only a few inches apart when seated. Of course, as newlyweds this was perfect. As I finished my last bite of a delicious meal, my new bride announced she had prepared a special dessert.

With great flair, she presented a cherry pie that rivaled any ever pictured in Southern Living Magazine. It was still warm, with a lattice style crust on top. She was obviously proud of her creation. After placing the pie on the little table, she served me a slice and mentioned that she had picked the cherries herself that morning from our tree. My mouth was watering. She waited for me to take my first bite. I put a huge forkful in my mouth. Immediately, I realized a serious flaw in the pie. As I chewed, it felt like I had a mouth full of marbles. Remember, our faces were only inches apart. I carefully pondered the best way to handle this little surprise. It was clear I was caught in a no win situation.

Carefully, I rolled the pie over to one side of my mouth and said, "Sweetheart, did you know that cherries have pits?"

She took a bite herself and quickly teared up. There, at our miniature table, she boo-hooed over the pits in the pie. You know there are times in a marriage when words will not comfort your mate. I did the best I could and said that other than the pits, the pie tasted really good. She was not comforted and threw the whole pie away in disgust. That was more than thirty years ago.

At the time, this surprise was not very funny. Of course, today it is a cherished memory that we laugh about. We have learned that surprises are a part of a marriage. Some will be welcomed, and some not so much. But they can sure make for some excitement as you learn about the one you love. Today I'm thankful for that cherry tree and the pie I never ate.

The Magnolia Tree / Photo by Benny Graves

# Chapter 23

## Sacrifice

In the still of the evening, the sweet fragrance of magnolia blossoms drifts to me in the thick summer air as I sit out back of my house on a worn wooden bench. The delicate aroma reminds me of my sweetheart, my love, my wife of over thirty years. I know she loves me deeply; the magnolia tree serves as a living reminder.

It's a lovely Southern Magnolia. Lush, dark glossy leaves form plush layers of green from top to bottom, creating a most pleasing symmetrical shape. While not a huge tree at twenty-eight feet in height, it has grown steadily with the passing years. In the early summer, the dark waxy leaves frame gorgeous white blooms, which open as big as saucers—elegant, ivory colored blossoms, the essence of which southern artists have strived for generations to capture on canvas.

She was fresh out of graduate school, a certified pediatric audiologist, trained by the best of the best at Vanderbilt University. An opportunity to work at Magnolia Speech School in Jackson, Mississippi, was offered and accepted. It was her dream job, the type of work she would have gladly done for free. She became part of a team of professionals dedicated to helping infants and young children with all types of hearing impairments. A gifted audiologist, she made a difference in the lives of countless families as they faced the uncertainties of their precious children's hearing and speech disorders. She was young, energetic, and went the extra mile every day for her young patients and their families. She loved them all, and they loved her back. It was a special time.

During this early part of her career, we fell in love and married. She split time in the first years of our marriage between living and working at Magnolia and being with me on the farm two hours away in rural Mississippi.  A few years later, as we talked about having children, she chose to leave her dream job and work at a University hearing center closer to our home. It was a gut-wrenching decision. Many tears were shed. Together we grieved her leaving the school she adored.

To commemorate that magical time at Magnolia Speech School, we planted a young magnolia tree behind our house on the farm.

It has been over thirty years since she left that wonderful first job. Together, we have nurtured two beautiful daughters and helped them grow into strong, independent young women. My wife is an amazing mother.  She has walked beside me every step of the way as we raised our children in a small Mississippi town. I am honored beyond words to be on this amazing journey of life with her. Like this special magnolia tree, our love grows ever deeper, stronger, richer with the passing of time.

Every now and then, I still catch her looking far away out the kitchen window of our home. Without asking, I know she is thinking of those sweet hearing impaired children she helped long ago and the dream job she left behind. She and I both know the deep sacrifice she made years ago to be with the one she loved. I don't take it lightly. I never will.

Not far from the back door of our home, there grows a beautiful Southern Magnolia tree. Its sweet fragrance comes to me in the still of the evening.

"They had buried him under our elm tree, they said-yet this was not totally true.
For he really lay buried in my heart."

**Willie Morris, My Dog Skip**

The Yard Tree / Photo by Benny Graves

# Chapter 24

## The Essence of Life

My new bride and I cleaned up the old empty farmhouse built by my Grandfather and moved into it to live the first few years of our marriage. We had only the essentials. Those were some special times as we worked together to make our way in the world. After three years, we decided to take a chance and build a new home just a stone's throw from the back door of the old house. Plans were drafted and discussed at length. We selected a building site on a little crest of land near a fine young pecan tree. I purposely laid out the house foundation so this particular tree would grace our yard only a few feet from the corner of our front porch. The house was built, and the young tree grew right along with our family. It has served us well as our favorite "yard tree."

Today, many years later, as I relax on the porch sipping a cold glass of sweet tea, I think of all the things our yard tree has shared with us through the years.

- Little girls laughing while swinging in a homemade swing hung from the tree's sturdy lower limb—they flew high in the summer breeze, free to dream

- Burying our beloved Sunny dog nearby

- Countless passes of an old riding lawn mower cutting green grass to perfection…again and again and again

- The stranded kitten crying from high in the tree, carefully rescued by my hands, making my family happy below

- Teaching kids how to catch fireflies with bare hands on lazy summer evenings under its branches during that magical moment somewhere between light and dark

- Cold watermelons cut with anticipation and shared among family and friends on the Fourth of July

- Barefoot children giggling as they created castles in the sandbox nestled under its shady protection

- Serving as "Home Base" during fun games of hide- and- seek for breathless players

- Raccoons and the occasional possum being startled at night and scurrying up the tree to escape from our sight

- We were awed by the harvest moon rising slowly on the eastern horizon, big and round, framed by its branches

- Our special handmade Christmas star hanging from the lower branch of the tree with care—in the darkness, it glowed with colored lights, bringing cheer to all

- Excited children making snow angels and funny snowmen under its snow-covered branches

- Colorful songbirds perching on its branches posing like Audubon paintings

- Vivid yellow spring daffodils blooming at the base of its trunk

- A wayward kite getting caught in the highest branches, of course

- Photographs being made each Easter after church under its watchful eye

- Family and friends visiting on the nearby porch, slowly rocking, telling stories, and laughing—wishing time could stand still.

As I sit here on my front porch, replaying these scenes over in my mind, I realize that the tree and I have shared experiences that are the essence of what life is all about. We both know that life is not really about material things at all. The yard tree and I have been blessed to enjoy a rich life filled with what is truly important.

Black Cherry / Photo by Benny Graves

# Chapter 25

## The Heart of a Tree

The heart of a Black Cherry tree is different. It is supposed to be hard. I have discovered that there is much to appreciate about a hard heart.

It all began when I was in my early twenties. I was working part time with the U.S. Forest Service and going to college. As part of my job, I learned about different species of wood, their properties, and uses. I became intrigued with black cherry trees, known for their rich, dark reddish-brown heartwood.   Black cherry wood, I discovered, was preferred by master craftsmen for making some of the most beautiful and durable furniture and cabinetry known in America. Furniture made from this tree was gorgeous. I started thinking about finding and cutting a tree or two and storing up some cherry lumber for use in my future dream home.

A young buddy of mine, who was a logger by trade, overheard me talking about my cherry wood idea and offered to help me cut some trees and haul them to a local sawmill. The search was on to find some trees big enough to cut for logs. I thought there might be some mature black cherry trees growing along the creeks on our farm property and asked Dad if I could cut a few. He didn't understand my sudden obsession with cherry wood but gave me his approval.

With his blessing, I combed the entire farm and was tickled to locate ten trees big enough and straight enough to make logs. My friend showed up with his log truck and loader, and we went to work with our chainsaws felling these trees. By sundown, we had filled his truck up with a heavy load of straight logs. The next day, we traveled to a small local sawmill a few miles out in the county and met the owner. He was an older man who walked with a limp. When we shook hands, I noticed his calloused right hand was missing a finger. Fortunately, we hit it off, and he agreed to saw my logs into one-inch boards.

A few weeks later, the sawmill man called and said my lumber was ready. I borrowed a sixteen-foot, flat-bed trailer and headed that way. When I arrived, I couldn't believe how much lumber the cherry logs cut out. I quickly realized it was going to take multiple trips with my little trailer to transport this large stack of lumber. I dug deep into my overall pockets to pay him for sawing up my logs. He charged me 65 cents a board foot.

At the time, it seemed like a lot to pay, but now I know he gave me quite a deal. Before I left, the mill owner made a point of telling me that it was good quality cherry lumber and that it had a "lot of heart." At the time, I didn't understand what he was talking about, but I thanked him and hurried on. I loaded up my trailer with a heavy load and tied the lumber down tight with some straps.

As soon as I pulled out onto the highway, tragedy struck. I was driving down the first hill when suddenly, the trailer started fishtailing wildly all over the road. Before I could blink, my pickup jerked across the highway and into the opposite lane. I panicked and stomped on the brakes as hard as I could. My brakes were useless because the heavy load of lumber was now in control. I prayed to God above with my eyes wide open as the load of lumber swerved me back and forth all over the highway. Tires were screeching and smoking the pavement. The terrifying ride seemed to last forever but, finally it was over. The truck and trailer slid to a stop on the shoulder of the road. I rested my head on the steering wheel in relief and waited for my racing heart to calm down.

I learned a valuable lesson that day: never pull a trailer with all the weight loaded to the back. A carload of good ole country boys stopped to help, and we restacked the lumber more to the front. I drove slowly home and never said a word to Dad about my wild ride. I stacked each green board one by one into the barn to dry. The width of the boards varied with a few as wide as 16 inches. Most of the planks consisted of solid heartwood. I laid spacers down between each layer to give it plenty of room to air dry. I didn't know when I would need the wood, but I knew it would take several years for the lumber to season enough to be useable.

Life happened, and I totally forgot about the black cherry wood. I happened to think about the stack of lumber when I was visiting home one Christmas about five years later. By this time, I was employed at my first job and living in the nearby college town. I decided it was time to upgrade the furniture in my apartment and use a few boards of the cherry wood to have some nice custom furniture made.

Someone recommended a young cabinetmaker in town who was just starting his own business. I visited his shop and showed him a sample of the cherry lumber. After drawing a rough sketch of the design I wanted on a scrap piece of cardboard, he agreed to make me a coffee table and two end tables. When I delivered the lumber to him, he handled each board and closely looked them over. I could tell he loved what he was seeing. Before I left, he commented that the black cherry lumber sure had "a lot of heart."

In a couple of months, my furniture was ready. When I arrived at his shop to pick it up, I was amazed at what he had created. The pieces were exquisite. He had transformed the rough planks into works of art. Under the touch of his skilled hands, the natural rich character of the heart cherry had come to life. I marveled at his attention to detail in the execution of each piece. This young man was destined to become a master cabinetmaker. Leaving his shop that day, I understood for the first time, what treasure lay hidden in my stack of cherry lumber back at the barn.

Later that same year, my Mother's older brother paid a visit to my family on the farm. Uncle Frank lived in Memphis and was recently retired. He had taken up woodworking and had crafted several pieces of furniture.

He happened to see my stack of cherry lumber and remarked that quality black cherry lumber was hard to find. He volunteered to make me a special piece of furniture if I would give him a few of the boards. I asked him what he was thinking of making; he just grinned and told me it would be a surprise. He left for Memphis with a load of boards hanging out of the back of his old El Camino.

Several months later, I traveled to his shop in Memphis to check out what he had built. First, he toured me through his house, showing me all the furniture he had created for his family. The walnut dining table, several grandfather clock cabinets, and a beautiful china cabinet were all extremely well made. I began to get excited. Uncle Frank was better at woodworking than I had thought. One by one, he proceeded to show me several of his intricately carved wooden birds displayed on various shelves. Finally, we walked out back to his shop. I was shocked to see a magnificent gun cabinet. Clearly, he had given careful thought to his surprise gift. He knew I loved hunting and would likely inherit several of the family shotguns. His workmanship was unbelievable. The luster of the polished cherry wood took my breath away.

Standing six and a half feet tall, the cabinet had an arched glass front door with padded gun slots. A handy ammunition storage area was built in at the base. Intricate scrollwork graced the top and bottom. It was obvious Uncle Frank was proud of this special gun cabinet he had created for his nephew. I was absolutely thrilled.

My appreciation for Uncle Frank's hand crafted surprise gift has only grown through the years. Today I understand more clearly his love. He chose to express it in hard cherry wood from the heart of a tree.

In 1984, one of my coworkers found out I had a stash of cherry lumber. Turns out, he made gunstocks for a hobby. He asked if I would give him some of my cherry wood and offered to pay me back by making something for my apartment. I was more than happy to fix him up with several boards. I really didn't expect much in return. Later, he presented me with a custom built, six-foot, full-length mirror, fully framed in my black cherry wood. His simple design of two raised layers of smooth wood with curved corners was executed to perfection. The dark natural grain of the hand polished frame enhanced the appearance of the large mirror. It hangs in our home today, a reminder of a favor among friends.

When my bride and I decided to build our home, I knew I wanted to include the cherry wood in some of the interior details of our home. Together we planned how and where to use it throughout the house. We were excited about the thought of having the warm rich wood from the farm's special black cherry trees surrounding us for the rest of our lives.

In order to use the rough lumber, I had to have it planed and a portion of it milled into tongue and groove. The mill operator said the heartwood was solid but would be hard to plane. In fact, it was so hard, the lumber had to be run through the machinery more than once. It was worth it, though. The end product turned out fantastic. I hauled the finished boards back home and once more stacked them back in the barn.

During the construction of our house's interior, a couple of old college friends came and spent the day, helping me cover one of the walls in our master bedroom with the tongue and groove cherry wood. It was a slow, tedious process because we had to predrill every nail hole due to the hardness of the wood. At the end of the day, the finished wall was strikingly beautiful and admired by all. I was surprised to discover that my college friends were so skilled. Their willingness to help me with the project was much appreciated.

We were able to use the cherry wood in several other accents in the very heart of our home. The wood is featured in our stone fireplace mantle, the staircase, and a custom-built bedroom dresser. As a final touch, I framed one of the roses that I gave to my wife when I proposed years ago. The frame is made of rich cherry wood from the heart of the tree. It is a constant reminder of our commitment to one another.

Today, the cherry wood in my home brings me great pleasure, but I enjoy much more thinking of the people who worked with this hard wood and played a part in making it come back to life. The logger, the crusty old saw mill operator, a young cabinet maker, a co-worker, the planer mill man, college friends, and a special uncle all saw its potential. Each man touched the very heart of a tree. They touched mine as well.

Photo by Andy McBee

"…bathed in the thick honey gold of the sun through encircling trees only just beginning to turn the muted metal colors of fall."
**Anne Rivers Siddons, Colony**

123

The Grafted Pecan Tree / Benny Graves

# Chapter 26

## Pass It On

After a passing summer rain shower, heavy limbs of green foliage gracefully hang low over my driveway. Pointed leaves drip big fat drops of pure water intercepted from the heavens above. They shower down and splatter all about me in perfect randomness. It is as if this particular pecan tree wants to make sure it gets my attention as I pass underneath. Yes, I notice. I appreciate this tree and the lesson it represents.

You see, it's all because of Lester.

Lester was a tall, slender man—long and lanky. I can still see him standing at ease with his hands on his hips, joking with me with his dry sense of humor. Lester, 20 years my senior, worked with me during the early years of my career as a regulatory plant pest inspector. He also was an avid beekeeper. The guy had a keen and observant eye for nature.

One year, Lester caught the grafting bug and grafted every wild pecan tree on his place. I tagged along with him one day, and he took time to teach me this amazing art of transformation. He encouraged me to use what I had learned and graft some wild pecan trees on my own family farm.

Lester helped me collect several pieces of bud wood from some select improved pecan varieties and showed me how to store them in my refrigerator. In early April, when the sap was flowing, I practiced this brand new skill on some of my trees. The first tree I attempted to graft was a small seedling pecan tree growing wild a few feet from the edge of our driveway. After sawing off the top from the young sapling, I cut three narrow flaps of bark around the edge of the knee-high stump. Then I carefully pulled them back and inserted three small, sharpened sticks of bud wood snug against the tree's cambium. All the wounds were coated with a liberal amount of Lester's beeswax. Next, the whole thing was encased with a clear plastic bag and secured tightly with a rubber band.

I waited.

Ten days later, signs of new growth appeared on the little twigs grafted onto the wild host tree. I was shocked that all three of the grafts took. I removed the plastic bag and watched the grafted sprouts over the next few weeks take off growing. I was so proud.

Within a few short years, the tree was producing nice long pecans of the Forkert variety. These nuts are known for their thin shells and great flavor. The squirrels and crows absolutely love them, too. I compete with these hungry creatures each and every year in a race to harvest these tasty nuts. The good news is that the tree has grown steadily for over 25 years, blessing us each year with more and more pecans to share.

Looking back, I deeply appreciate Lester taking the time to teach a young man the art of tree grafting. His selfless act of sharing his knowledge and encouragement lives on in this beautiful tree and is a living lesson of one man's kindness. This grafted tree reminds me to pass along the gifts of knowledge and kindness to the next generation. Lester, with his hands on his hips and a smile on his face, would approve.

Photo by istock.com/bennygraves

"It is difficult to realize how great a part of all that is cheerful and delightful
in the recollections  of our own life is associated with trees."

**Wilson Flagg, Extract from Beauty of Trees, Atlantic Monthly June, 1868**

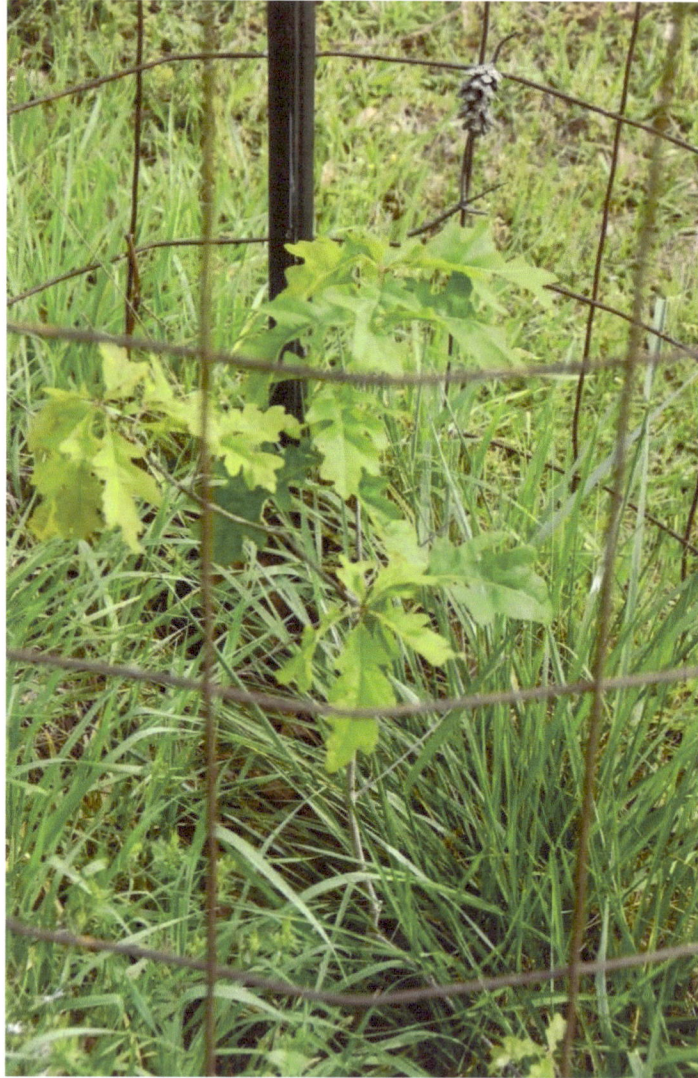

A Time to Plant Trees / Photo by Benny Graves

# Chapter 27

## Give Back to the Land

Young men cut down trees…. Old men plant trees.

Sometime in my mid- fifties, I determined I needed to plant some oak trees on the farm with the help of my two daughters. I felt this would be a good bonding activity.

Claire, our older daughter, was home from college for the Christmas holidays when I suggested we take a walk and plant some trees. I had purchased seedlings of Cherry Bark, Nutall, and Scarlet oaks that were less than two feet tall and no more than one-half inch in diameter, just right for planting. We grabbed a shovel and the dozen oak seedlings and headed out into the pastures to find just the right site. We placed three of them in the lot close behind the old dairy barn in a protected area. You see, foraging cows are a young tree's worst enemy. We planted the other young trees across the road around Buster's house, the old abandoned sharecropper's shack.

We laughed and talked that afternoon as we worked side by side carefully planting them in the cool, damp soil. Our time together in the fresh December air meant a lot to me.

Ten years later, these young oaks are 20 feet tall and growing fast. Claire is all grown up now and lives in the big city far away.  Whenever she visits home, she always checks on the progress of the trees we planted together. In her heart, she knows these trees represent a fun, shared experience with her father that only grows more special with time.

Later, I also made a point to plant three white oak seedlings with my younger daughter, Ellen. We had just finished draining and reworking the farm pond. Now full of water again, I could almost feel the pond begging for some shade trees. So I dug up three little white oak seedlings, each about a foot tall, from under some ancient trees located back in the big woods—the same big woods my dad found his three oak seedlings years ago for his home. On a sunny February day, with careful hands, Ellen helped me plant the trees in a little group just a few feet from the pond's edge. To protect the young trees from hungry cows, we built a wire cage around each one. Ellen was so proud of her hard work.

Today she loves to walk in the pasture down by the pond and enjoy her trees from time to time. In the last few years, she and I have pruned the weeds and briars back to give them unfettered room to grow. As the days turn into years, the three little trees continue to grow and are a sweet reminder of our shared bond with the land.

Planting young trees teaches us all the important lesson of giving back to the land, and by doing so, we give something forward to unknown generations yet to come. The thought of a person in the future pausing to appreciate a grove of magnificent old oaks planted by the hands of my daughters gives me deep satisfaction.

I hope these trees will be loved by others and that they, too, will experience the wisdom of trees.

"That's when I see it, there at the side of the road; a single, perfectly shaped cedar
or pine, not too short, not too tall, and I think, for just a second, that I wish I had a saw.
And I know that, for me and mine, it is truly Christmas, after all."

**Rick Bragg, Southern Living, O Christmas Tree**

131

The Burning Tree / Photo by Benny Graves

# Chapter 28

## Freedom

On a hot, sultry August afternoon, the western sky turned a dark, greenish black. A bad looking thunderstorm was brewing on the horizon and rolling toward our farm. The weather alert radio blared an announcement of a severe thunderstorm warning. Hail and strong winds could be expected. The storm struck our place at 4:15 pm. A ragged streak of lightning crashed nearby, and as the thunder shook the house, a gale of wind whipped across the landscape followed closely by a massive wall of rain mixed with hail. As our family hunkered down in the center of our home and prayed, a huge old water oak tree fell victim to this unbelievable force of nature.

After the storm had passed and the thunder and lightning had receded into the east, I walked out the back door to survey the damage. Looking through the fog rising from the melting hailstones, I saw in the distance the uprooted oak lying crushed to the ground. Though I had witnessed similar events of nature many times in my life, I must admit I felt an intense pang of grief to see this long familiar tree suddenly taken.

This broad majestic water oak was the tree whose low hanging limbs I sat on when I was just a boy. It allowed me to bounce up and down for hours--singing softly to myself. Later, my young daughters did the same. For years, this particular oak provided shade for the cows to rest from the midday heat. They loved to rub their backs on those same low limbs I used to ride. In the spring, I remember watching a colorful pair of redheaded woodpeckers making their nesting hole in a dead stub of a limb high among its branches. In winter, often a singular red-tailed hawk would sit high upon its bare branches watching and waiting for just the right moment to swoop down upon its next meal. For untold years, the oak stood upon the earth from which it was born. It stood in a quiet strength, with a glorious presence that captured the very spirit of the place. I miss this tree.

Sometime later, after the wet ground had dried up, I drove beside the fallen oak in my old truck. I cranked my heavy chainsaw and started the laborious process of cutting up the tree piece by piece. With the tree's own limbs, I built its funeral pyre.

On a clear summer day, a year later, I lay a lighted match to the dry remains of my old friend, the water oak. The tiny flame slowly, steadily grew. Within a few minutes, the hungry fire raged, snapping and popping against the broad trunk. I had to turn my back and walk away.

**\*\*\*\***

Five days later…

Seated on the tailgate of my old pickup, I watch as small glowing flames of fire lick the remaining carcass of the fallen oak. In the gathering twilight of a peaceful summer evening, my eyes track the plume of smoke as it rises upward, then levels off into a thin layer to drift slowly among the nearby trees. A lone tree once bound to the earth, felled by nature, is now forever set free to wander the skies. The smell of smoke becomes the smell of freedom for one proud tree.

For a few moments, in the late evening stillness, the pale smoke hangs suspended among the tops of the other trees on the farm, as if for one final farewell. This intimate scene of transfiguration lingers in my mind … and seeps deep into my soul.

# ACKNOWLEDGMENTS

Writing and publishing this book was an epic journey. Many people assisted me along the way.

First, I want say thanks to my family and friends, both living and dead, who furnished so many of these life experiences and rich memories. I appreciate your laughter and showing me how to enjoy life to its fullest. Your lives color these stories and give depth to the written words.

Andy McBee provided a stunning personal photograph for this book. He is such an accomplished photographer and an even better brother-in-law. Thank you also to Kim Strickland and Beth Ann Johnson for their excellent technical assistance.

Kim Coghlan of Coghlan Professional Writing Services guided me through the early stages of editing. You taught me so much.

I want to thank James L. Dickerson of Sartoris Literary Group for believing in this project. I appreciate the great work Sartoris performed during the designing and publishing of this book.

Special thanks to my daughters Ellen and Claire for their enthusiastic support. They give my life wings.

To my wife Deanie, thank you seems so inadequate. I couldn't have picked a better partner to dance with under the trees. During the creation of this book your encouragement, artistic vision and endless hours of editing kept me motivated to produce my best work. Thank you for always believing in me.

Finally, I would like to salute the trees I walk among daily on this little farm. The simple joy they bring is forever interwoven into my life.

# THE DANCE CARD

Tree measurements: C (measurements) / CS (crown spread) / H (height)

**Chapter 1: Three Oaks Still Stand**
Water Oak (*Quercus nigra*), 2015. C: 12ft. 4in. CS: 108ft. 9in. H: 101ft.

**Chapter 2:  Seven Sisters**
Pecan (*Carya Illinoensis*), 2015. C: 9ft. 7in. CS: 101ft. H: 105ft.

**Chapter 3:  Last Tree Before Home**
Sweetgum(*Liquidambar styraciflua*), 2015. C: 5ft. average of 4 trunks, CS: 71ft. H: 91ft.

**Chapter 4:  The Persimmon Tree**
Persimmon  ( *Diospyros virginiana*), 2015. C: 3ft. 5in. CS: 28ft. H: 73ft.

**Chapter 5: The Last Tree Standing**
Pecan (*Carya illinoensis* var. *stuart*), 2015. C: 6ft. 9in. CS: 64ft. H: 88ft.

**Chapter 6: The Hickory Tree and the Gap**
Mockernut Hickory (*Carya tomentosa*), 2015. C: 7ft. CS: 59ft. 6in. H: 73ft.

**Chapter 7: The Sycamore Tree**
American Sycamore (Platanus occidentalis),2017. C: 5ft. 4in. CS: 43ft. H: 65ft.

**Chapter 8: The Sweetbay Tree**
Sweetbay (Magnolia virginiana), 2017. C: 8ft. 11in. CS: 52ft. H: 62ft.

**Chapter 9: The Christmas Tree**
Eastern red cedar (Juniperus virginiana), 2017. C: 3in. CS: 4ft. H: 9ft.

**Chapter 10: The Pear Tree**
Pear (*Pyrus communis*), 2015. C: 4ft. 11in. CS: 30ft. 2in. H: 34ft.

**Chapter 11: The Lookout Tree**
Post Oak (*Quercus stellata*), 2015. C: 6ft. 11in. CS: 41ft. H: 49ft.

**Chapter 12: The Tree That Saw It Al**
Sweetgum (*Liquidambar styraciflua*), 2015. C: 8ft. 7in. CS: 64ft. H: 97ft.

**Chapter 13: The Big Oak Tree**
Willow Oak (*Quercus phellos*), 2015. C: 17ft. 4in. CS: 116ft. H: 111ft.

**Chapter 14: The Lone Oak**
Southern Red Oak (Quercus falcata), 2015. C: 15 ft. 4 in. CS: 97 ft. H: 80 ft.

**Chapter 15: The Twice Struck Tree**
Loblolly Pine (*Pinus taeda*), 2015. C: 9ft. CS: 54ft. H: 96ft.

**Chapter 16: The Inez Pine**
Loblolly Pine (*Pinus taeda*), 2015. C: 9ft. 9in. CS: 56ft. H: 94ft.

**Chapter 17: The Holly Tree**
American Holly (*Ilex opaca*), 2015. C: 2ft. 5in. average of 9 trunks, CS: 31ft. H: 37ft.

**Chapter 18: I Hear the Acorns Fall**
White Oak (*Quercus alba*), 2015. C: 10ft. 10in. CS: 75ft. H: 83ft.

**Chapter 19: Out of Destruction**
Water Oak (*Quercus nigra*), 2015. C: 2ft. 3in. CS: 28ft. 10in. H: 39ft. 10in.

**Chapter 20: The Leaning Tree**
Slippery Elm (Ulmu rubra), 2015. C: 6ft.6in. CS: 73ft. H: 56ft.

Chapter 21: The Sassafras Grove
Sassafras (Sassafras albidum), 2017. C: 1ft. 11in. CS: 21ft. H: 44ft.

Chapter 22: The Cherry Pie Tree
Cherry (Prunus cerasum), 1984. C: 1ft. 4in. CS: 15ft. H: 16ft.

Chapter 23: The Magnolia Tree
Southern Magnolia (*Magnolia grandiflora*), 2015. C: 1ft. 8in. CS: 20ft. H: 28ft.

Chapter 24: The Yard Tree
Pecan (*Carya illinoensis*),2015. C: 7ft. 4in. CS: 81ft. 8in. H: 75ft.

Chapter 25: Black Cherry
Black Cherry (Prunus serotina), 2017. C: 3ft. 4in. CS: 40ft. H: 52ft.

Chapter 26: The Grafted Pecan Tree
Pecan (*Carya illinoensis* var. *forkert*), 2015. C: 4ft. 3in. CS: 42ft. 5in. H: 46ft.

Chapter 27: A Time to Plant Trees
White Oak (*Quercus alba*), 2015. C: 1in. CS: 2ft. H: 4ft. 9in.

www.ingramcontent.com/pod-product-compliance
Lightning Source LLC
Chambersburg PA
CBHW041652260326

41914CB00017B/1620